"Highly recommended. A sparkling book that is not only easy to read and digest in one day but also packed with useful tips. Applicable to everyone, with clear do's and don'ts for all leadership styles. This book is a must-read for skeptics as well as believers that agile can lead to sustainable success."

—**CARLO VIVALDI**, Co-Chief Operating Officer, UniCredit

"No matter where your company is on its journey to agile, *Doing Agile Right* serves as a useful guidebook for senior management teams. The authors bring decades of experience and perspective to demystifying an often misunderstood topic."

—**RITCH ALLISON**, CEO, Domino's Pizza

"Business leaders responsible for leading transformative change will benefit greatly from *Doing Agile Right.* The specific examples and empirical evidence show how agile helps a company innovate and evolve."

—**PAUL SANFORD**, Senior Vice President, Solutions Delivery, Cigna

"*Doing Agile Right* lays out the steps organization-wide that allow traditional companies to perform software development like digital natives. CIOs and their business partners in the digital transformation journey will find this book an invaluable road map."

—**MICHELLE A. ROUTH**, Chief Information Officer, CARE USA

"Having experienced as a practitioner many of the challenges of large-scale agile transformation, I value this unfiltered view of the journey to agility. Every step has practical examples highlighting do's and don'ts."

—**PRAT VEMANA**, Senior Vice President and Chief Digital Officer, Kaiser Permanente

DOING AGILE RIGHT

Darrell Rigby • Sarah Elk • Steve Berez

BAIN & COMPANY, INC.

DOING AGILE RIGHT

Transformation Without Chaos

HARVARD BUSINESS REVIEW PRESS • BOSTON, MASSACHUSETTS

Library of Congress Cataloging-in-Publication Data

Names: Rigby, Darrell, author. | Berez, Steve, author. | Elk, Sarah, author.
Title: Doing agile right : transformation without chaos / by Darrell Rigby,
    Steve Berez, and Sarah Elk (Bain & Company, Inc.).
Description: Boston, MA : Harvard Business Review Press, [2020] | Includes index.
Identifiers: LCCN 2019054607 | ISBN 9781633698703 (hardcover) |
    ISBN 9781633698710 (ebook)
Subjects: LCSH: Agile project management. | Success in business.
Classification: LCC HD69.P75 R33 2020 | DDC 658.4/06—dc23
LC record available at https://lccn.loc.gov/2019054607

ISBN: 978-1-63369-870-3
eISBN: 978-1-63369-871-0

To those who share our belief that great businesses should produce better people—and to the colleagues and clients who make our own work and growth so fulfilling.

Contents

DOING
AGILE
RIGHT

Introduction

THE UNBALANCED COMPANY

Agile—the business philosophy that relies on fast-moving, self-managing teams for innovation—has officially entered the mainstream of corporate management. Tour almost any large company these days and you will find scores of agile teams working to improve customer experiences and business processes. John Deere has used agile methods to develop new machines, USAA to transform its customer service, and 3M to run a major merger integration. Bosch—a global supplier of technology and services with more than 400,000 associates—has adopted agile principles to guide a step-by-step reshaping of the company. Digital natives such as Amazon, Netflix, and Spotify have incorporated agile methods into a wide range of innovation activities. Meanwhile, agile has virtually taken over IT departments, themselves the source of countless innovations. At last count, 85 percent of software developers use agile techniques in their work.[1]

The reasons for agile's rapid spread are neither obscure nor surprising. Most big companies find it difficult to innovate. They are weighted down by the structures and procedures of bureaucracy. Agile liberates the innovative spirit that so many organizations stifle. It helps companies reshape both what they offer their customers and how they operate internally. It transforms the work environment, making people's jobs more rewarding.

These are grand claims, but the data support them. Study after study find conclusively that agile teams are far more successful at innovation than teams that work in traditional fashion. Improvements come rapidly and at less expense. Satisfaction and engagement among employees rise. Moreover, companies can implement agile without the need to spin off separate business units or hide skunkworks from hierarchies. They can deploy agile teams in any business or function that might benefit from them, including corporate headquarters. Once they have learned the basics, they can scale agile, establishing hundreds of individual teams or teams of teams to tackle large projects. Saab's aeronautics business created more than one hundred agile teams operating across software, hardware, and fuselage for its Gripen fighter jet—a $43 million item that is certainly one of the most complex products in the world. Military analyst Jane's has deemed the Gripen the world's most cost-effective military aircraft.

So agile is spreading, and agile teams are mostly achieving their objectives. It looks like encouraging progress toward an appealing vision. Is there anything wrong with this picture?

Certainly there's nothing wrong with the basic idea. We are business consultants, and we have seen the power and potential of agile in hundreds of companies around the globe. We have helped many of these companies implement agile. We count ourselves among its biggest fans.

But as with so many good ideas, the practice sometimes belies the promise. Agile has spread so rapidly that it threatens to spin out of control. Along with the companies that use it effectively are those that misunderstand or misuse the ideas. They may be egged on by some zealot who promises the world. They may sign on to an agile transformation before they know anything about what such an effort might entail. They may use agile terminology to camouflage distinctly nonagile objectives.

The outcome of these misuses in many companies is chaos rather than constructive change. But the damage is greater than any one company's experience. When agile is done wrong, it almost always leads to lousy results. Lousy results lead to nervous customers, dissatisfied employees, activist investors, and a push to replace the management team. Replacement managers are understandably skeptical of any strategies that got the prior regime fired. They are likely to clean house, disband agile teams, and (probably) launch a round of layoffs. It's a version of Gresham's law: bad agile drives out good. If that happens too often, agile will be discredited—and the business world will be back where it started, with top-heavy bureaucratic corporations struggling hopelessly to keep up with brash upstarts and rapidly changing markets.

So in this book we want to bring agile down to earth, to separate Agile Done Right from Agile Done Wrong. Here, in the introduction, we'll focus on the wrongheadedness, the potholes and pitfalls, the ways in which companies have already misunderstood or misused agile. We hope that the lessons and cautionary tales will inoculate you against the idea that agile is some kind of magic quick fix. But we'll also introduce some of the ideas that inform the chapters that follow—chapters that will tell you how to do agile right. We'll provide a road map to these chapters, and we'll summarize the research that underlies the book. Doing agile right may take more time and experimentation than doing it wrong—but it's the only way to get the results that the philosophy promises.

Doing Agile Wrong

In the movie *The Princess Bride*, the swordsman Inigo Montoya famously chides the cunning Vizzini, "You keep using that word. I do not think it means what you think it means." So it is with agile. Executives often fail to understand how agile operates and where and why it has succeeded. That doesn't stop them from throwing around the terminology or from making assumptions about agile that simply aren't true.

Some of these misunderstandings reflect the fact that agile methods—especially those relating to expanding the scope and scale of agile innovation teams—are still relatively new, and many business leaders haven't yet learned much about them. It's common to hear, for example, that agile is great but only for technology-based innovations and the IT departments that generate those innovations. This will come as news to National Public Radio, which used agile methods to create new programs; to the people developing the Gripen fighter jet or Haier's home appliances; and to the many companies using agile to reshape their supply chains. Historically, to be sure, agile has spread most rapidly in IT. But it is widely and successfully used in many other contexts, some of which have only minor technology-based components.

Other failings, though we hate to say it, reflect a measure of cynicism on the part of corporate leaders. Consider the clever press release that Edward S. Lampert, CEO of Sears, issued in 2017: "In addition to the cost reduction target announced today, we continue to assess our overall operating model and capital structure to become a more agile . . . and innovative retailer focused on member experience."[2] *Agile* in this context is a euphemism for layoffs. And Lampert isn't alone. Every month we receive more requests for proposals that begin something like this: "The project objective (should you choose to accept it) is to reduce operating expenses by 30 percent this year while transforming the organization to agile ways of working and digital technology."

The issuers of these requests don't understand that there are basic inconsistencies between large, chaotic layoffs and agile. For one thing, large layoffs tend to happen in batches driven by precipitous restructurings or annual budgeting cycles. This is diametrically opposed to the continuous learning and adaptation processes prescribed by agile. For another, senior executives typically go behind closed doors to plan the layoffs, emerging with new structures and fixed targets. This is inconsistent with the agile principle of empowering people closest to the work to identify improvement opportunities. Worst of all, leaders who try to marry agile with layoffs inadvertently role-model antiagile behaviors. They create predictive, command-and-control events rather than agile, test-and-learn cultures. Moreover, research shows that large layoffs increase risk aversion and slow innovation. People scramble to learn new jobs. They battle for control of key operations, no matter what the organization chart says. They do everything possible to make sure they will have a chair next year, when the music is likely to stop once again. Mostly, they try to do the same things they know how to do, but with fewer people. This is not an environment in which agile can flourish.

But then there is a different kind of wrongheadedness, not generated by complete ignorance or cynicism. These misuses are propagated by well-meaning agile partisans. They are sold to leadership teams who badly want their companies to become nimbler and more innovative but who don't really understand how agile operates. In our work with hundreds of companies launching thousands of agile initiatives, we commonly find three toxic mistakes.

Agile, Agile, Everywhere

Some agile gurus pitch the approach as a panacea that must replace bureaucracy everywhere—in every company, in every business unit, in every function.

Consider a company that we'll call MagicAgile. (This is a real company, but we don't want to identify it because our conversations with its leaders were confidential.) The people at this company wanted to be like digital disruptors such as Spotify, the music streaming company that is well known for its agile innovation teams. So MagicAgile launched agile teams throughout its organization. It redesigned office spaces to create more open work areas. It innovated around customer and employee experiences. Through the eyes of agile evangelists, MagicAgile looked like a poster child—or at least it did if you ignore the fact that it lost about half of its market value in 2018 and early 2019 (or if you can claim with a straight face that things would have been even worse without the transformation, or that shareholder value doesn't matter anyway). But in candid meetings with the leadership team of MagicAgile, we heard nearly every executive voice frustrations with their less visible results. They said things like this: "Agile has created a leadership problem. We have no discipline or alignment. This is chaos." "We went too far. Everybody is talking about servant leadership and psychological safety. Nobody is allowed to use the word *manager*, and all managers have gone into hiding." "Responsibilities for P&Ls are getting confused." "Our leaders are criticized and ignored when we try to provide strategic guidance to our business units." "Agile became the objective. We are praying at the altar of a false church."

What the agile-everywhere zealots fail to understand is the time-tested virtues of bureaucracy—in some places and contexts. The same bureaucracy now so widely reviled as antithetical to change and innovation was itself one of the greatest innovations in the history of business. Hierarchical authority, specialized division of labor, and standard operating procedures—the hallmarks of the bureaucratic method—enabled companies to grow far larger than they had ever been. The principles of bureaucracy were taught as good management practices in business schools and corporate training programs. Companies learned the virtues of predictability and planning. Strong bureaucrats rose to the tops of their organizations.

Today we understand bureaucracy's limitations. The great German sociologist Max Weber, who was the first to offer a systematic description of bureaucracy and who well understood its efficiencies, famously warned that it could create a soulless "iron cage" that trapped people in dehumanizing organizations and limited their potential.[3] He was right: most people today work in bureaucracies, and most feel disengaged from their work. The widespread appeal to young people of start-ups and small businesses, as compared with careers spent climbing corporate ladders, reflects this flaw. Then, too, bureaucracies are terrible at innovating. A bureaucracy works when its organizational tasks—what to deliver and how to deliver it—are clear, stable, and predictable. Innovation, by definition, meets none of these criteria. These limitations have contributed to bureaucracy's bad reputation and to the growth of antibureaucratic approaches such as agile.

And yet. Consider the adverse consequences of encouraging wide variation, on-the-spot experimentation, and decentralized decision making—all hallmarks of agile—in areas such as food or drug safety, antidiscrimination and harassment policies, accounting standards, aircraft safety, quality controls, and manufacturing standards. Every company has to run its business, getting standardized products out the door and delivering predictable services to customers. Every company needs bureaucratic structures and procedures, including hierarchical approvals, specialized division of labor, and standard operating procedures, to do exactly that.

The challenge, in short, is not to replace bureaucracy with agile everywhere but to find the right balance between the two. Every company must run its businesses. It must be good at *operations*. Every company must also change the business, continuously introducing not just new products and services but new operating methods and procedures. It must be good at *innovating*. Although these tasks require different skills, they are not enemies. They are complementary, interdependent, mutually beneficial capabilities that need each other to survive. Insufficient focus on innovation leads to a static enterprise that will fail to adapt to changing conditions. Insufficient emphasis on operations creates chaos—poor quality, high costs, and dangerous risks to customers and to the business.

Most large companies today have tilted too far toward bureaucracy, starving innovation. They have created static organizations committed to delivering predictable results. This is why agile is so popular. But the solution isn't to tip the scale all the way in the other direction. Rather, it is to stick with bureaucratic rules and hierarchies where they are appropriate, humanizing them as much as possible, and at the same time to instill a healthy admixture of agile wherever it is appropriate. That may sound simple, but it isn't. Agile and bureaucracy are like oil and vinegar: they are good together, but they don't mix easily. (Sometimes the two act more like nitric acid and glycerol: they lead to explosions.) Agile teams thrive on doing things quickly. The teams try out new ideas, often before the ideas are fully formed, and test them with prospective customers. They don't respect red tape, and they don't follow detailed plans. If such teams are to thrive in an organization, they need a lot of freedom and a lot of support. Bureaucracies, of course, are just the opposite: they thrive on—indeed, require—tight control. They want to know exactly what a team has done so far, what it plans to do for the next twelve months, and how much it is all going to cost. To a traditional bureaucracy, agile teams can feel like foreign bodies infecting the organism. Like T cells in an immune system, bureaucrats often see their job as eliminating the infection or at least limiting its damage.

In a truly agile enterprise, bureaucracy and innovation become partners. They create a system where both elements improve and where people in each camp collaborate to generate superior results. We'll show how to harmonize the two in this book.

Let's Have You Folks Do Agile

Frederick Winslow Taylor claimed to take bureaucratic management from an art to a science. His stopwatch studies are classics in the annals of business. His 1911 book, *The Principles of Scientific Management*, outlined four fundamental tenets: (1) managers plan work, and workers do it; (2) managers scientifically analyze the most efficient ways for workers to work; (3) managers scientifically select and train the right workers for the right jobs; and (4) managers rigorously supervise workers as they perform tasks.[4] At the time, Taylor's methods drew harsh criticism for treating humans like machines. But his approach caught on, and indeed it has long outlived him—even today, many companies have plenty of managers and executives who are Taylorists at heart. And when Taylorists try to implement agile, bad things happen.

Here's how it often works: Top leaders plan the agile transformation for their subordinates, not for themselves. They create a high-powered program management office to drive the change. This office generates detailed budgets, milestones, and execution road maps, complete with Gantt charts and stoplight reporting systems, to ensure conformance to plans. It creates a slew of agile teams, typically led by Taylorists who are fresh from two days of training. When one of the teams registers a success, however tenuous, the program office broadcasts it, in hopes of convincing both internal and external audiences that the initiative is working precisely as planned. Meanwhile, the leadership team continues operating much as before, supervising and (often) micromanaging their subordinates, a group that now includes members of agile teams. These leaders frequently tell the teams not only what to do but how to do it. After all, isn't that the job of an executive?

But agile dies on the vine when it is micromanaged from above. All the agile language about self-management, testing and learning, and so forth begins to feel like a sham. Anyway, the tools of top-down management don't work in an agile environment. Benchmarks turn out to be worthless outside their unique contexts. Predictive plans are usually wrong, because they fail to recognize or adapt to unpredictable system dynamics. We use a survey called the Bain Agility Quotient to diagnose the health and maturity of agile initiatives throughout an organization. Wherever the Taylorist approach thrives, the perception gaps between senior executives and team members are large. Senior executives describe the company's agile initiatives as successful and satisfying. Team members, who are closer to the action, describe them as disappointing and frustrating, not much different from traditional task forces. At first we thought the executives must be lying, but we soon discovered they are merely out of touch. They are so distant from the agile work that they only know what subordinates tell them, and subordinates tell them only what they want to hear.

To be sure, some agile teams have succeeded even in Taylorist enterprises. They stay under executives' radar, and they thrive in spite of senior management rather than because of it. But a true agile transformation requires the active involvement and support of the company's leaders. Senior executives who really want to scale agile will do better by showing others how to do it than by sending subordinates off to training seminars. They themselves must understand agile, love it, and use its methods in teams of their own. Gandhi famously said, "If we could change ourselves, the tendencies in the world would also change." So it is with agile.

Agile as a Quick Fix

A few companies, facing urgent strategic threats and in need of radical change, have pursued big-bang, everything-at-once agile transformations in some units. For example, in 2015 ING Netherlands anticipated rising customer demand for digital solutions and increasing incursions by new digital competitors known as fintechs. The management team decided to move aggressively. It dissolved the organizational structures of its most innovative functions, including IT development, product management, channel management, and marketing—essentially abolishing everyone's job. Then it created small agile "squads" and required nearly 3,500 employees to reapply for 2,500 redesigned positions on those squads. About 40 percent of the people filling the positions had to learn new jobs, and all had to profoundly change their mindsets.[5]

Experience has revealed countless problems with this approach. It confuses and traumatizes the organization. People aren't sure where to go or what to do. It assumes that thousands of individuals, most of whom have no experience or knowledge of agile, will suddenly understand and work according to its principles. Although radicalized converts have publicly touted their success, overall results frequently failed to meet unrealistic promises; stock prices (including ING's) have often declined, sometimes by 30 percent or more. Behind closed doors, these executives and their subordinates are more balanced, typically offering assessments that sound something like this: "Our leaders and culture were not ready for such radical change. The more we recited conventional clichés about 'ripping off the Band-Aid' and 'burning the boats' of retreat, the more we believed them. But nobody in our senior team had ever worked in an agile environment. We did not foresee or plan for the unintended consequences. Worse yet, we lost some great people who were branded as obstructionists for trying to point out those consequences. Our approach to agility was not very agile."

More common than big bangs in the quick-fix department is the bureaucrat's favorite innovation tool: copying others. Of course, executives use nicer names for it—benchmarking, competitive intelligence, or becoming a so-called fast follower—but it all boils down to copying. A favorite template is Spotify, well known for its original agile lexicon of squads, tribes, guilds, and the like. Some companies even find themselves copying some other company that originally copied Spotify.

The logic of copying is seductive. Agile pioneers like Spotify have spent years learning and applying agile principles. Why not replicate that success in six months? Particularly enticing is the idea that all you have to do is copy the pioneer's organization structure and office design. If you change the boxes and the layouts, you will surely force changes in how people approach their work. Changing the ways of working, in turn, will change outputs and outcomes. What could possibly go wrong?

Well, let us count the ways. For one, human organizations (like human bodies) are complex systems, which means that variables interact differently in different environments. Medications that work for some patients may be harmful to people with different genetics, genders, ages, or foods in their system. Managers who attempt to paste the structures of innovation departments at one company onto the entire enterprise of another are bound to produce unintended consequences. Spotify itself is sophisticated enough to understand this. It designed its engineering model to match its unique culture, capitalizing on the trust and collaboration inherent in the department's values. Spotify's engineering teams have fewer interdependencies than at most organizations because of its modular products and technology architecture. So would-be copiers with product lines requiring close coordination of interdependencies often end up with tribe structures that create chaos. Spotify people adamantly warn that its engineering model is constantly evolving and should not be copied by other companies or even by other areas within Spotify. Still, the copying continues.

A second problem with copying org charts: Too often, companies unintentionally destroy accountabilities in their business units. They create shiny new silos of agile teams that are every bit as challenging to integrate as functional silos ever were. General managers who once felt like CEOs of their units suddenly find themselves without the authority to make tough trade-offs. The financial performance of one company's credit card business, for example, deteriorated significantly when key revenue and cost levers were distributed among many different tribes beyond the influence of the business unit leader. Agile teams have to support properly defined business units—units that are accountable for meaningful P&Ls. They can't bypass or compromise those units without jeopardizing accountabilities.

Third, matrix management brings unexpected complexities. Agile teams are cross-functional teams. Cross-functional teams, by definition, require matrix organizations. Matrices may look easy on paper, but we often find ourselves cleaning up companies that launched hundreds of agile teams and never anticipated the inevitable turf battles. Who owns the teams? Who can launch additional teams? Should there be separate organization units for technology-based agile teams (sometimes called product teams) and all other innovation teams? Who funds the teams, how will decision rights work, how will teams be measured and rewarded—on and on. These details are invisible on organization charts. They are easy to overlook and impossible to copy from others.

But the worst problem is that copycats have not learned the keystone of agile success: the ability to continuously learn, evolve, improve, and grow. In trying to shortcut the process, they fail to develop skills for adapting, customizing, and harmonizing all the elements of an operating system. Agile transitions are never-ending journeys, not copy-and-paste projects. People need time to create—and get accustomed to—a new operating model. Predicting exactly how any given change will affect the organization is hard, so testing, learning, and step-by-step scaling are essential.

Agile methods, like all other management tools, have strengths and weaknesses. They do not eliminate problems. When used properly, in appropriate situations, they trade potentially disastrous problems for preferable problems. Small, autonomous agile teams are happier, faster, and more successful, but they also require more coordination and more frequent planning and funding cycles. Agile teams eliminate layers of hierarchy, but fewer layers mean fewer title changes and less frequent promotions. Failure to anticipate and address such challenges will confuse and disappoint team members. The best approach is not to choose agile over all other management approaches but to learn when, where, and how to use it in combination with other tools. This is consistent with what Aristotle, more than 2,300 years ago, called "finding the golden mean." It is also a practical path to achieving what others have called ambidextrous organizations using contingency theory and Theory Y philosophies.

Doing Agile Right: A Road Map of This Book

Back in 2001, after software developers had practiced so-called lightweight development methods for about a decade, a group of seventeen practitioners gathered to share what they had learned about better methods. They renamed the lightweight approaches *agile* and created a simple set of principles to define the process. Their Manifesto for Agile Software Development helped hundreds of thousands of individual software teams adopt and apply agile practices. Today, as companies have wrestled with agile at scale for about a decade, we're in a similar situation: we now have enough experience to analyze new patterns of success and failure. So we need to weed out the noxious misunderstandings and misuses of scaling agile before bad agile drives out good—before this powerful philosophy joins business process reengineering and quality circles on the scrap heap of management manias. It's time to bring more sanity, practicality, and balance to the agile movement. That's the purpose of this book. We want agile to become a valuable and practical tool rather than one more frustrating fad. We believe that agile mindsets and methods can make people in an organization far happier and more successful. We want readers to look back on their agile transitions in five to ten years with a sense of pride and fulfillment rather than disappointment and remorse.

Who will benefit from the book? We have several kinds of readers in mind. We want to help senior executives of large companies—especially large companies mired in bureaucracy—close the chasm between their bureaucratic malaise and their agile aspirations. We want to help those who are just beginning their agile journey to avoid the mistakes we have just described, and we want to help them develop agile attitudes and habitual behaviors that will create sustainable results rather than chaos. If a company has already begun its agile journey on the wrong foot, we hope to help it recognize and escape the pitfalls before it's too late. Of course, we suspect that agile team members—and other employees who collaborate with agile teams—will also use this book to improve their performance (and maybe share it with some antiagile bosses). And we expect that start-ups already steeped in agile practices will use it to build balanced agile enterprises as they scale their success. In all these cases, our purpose is to help people build agile habits that will improve their results and increase their happiness.

For all these readers, we have tried to write a compact guidebook that time-starved businesspeople can actually read. We designed each chapter as a logical and sustainable step in the journey to an agile enterprise.

Chapter 1: How Agile Really Works. Few executives have ever watched an agile team in action. Fewer yet have actively participated in one, and almost none have actually led one. Without that kind of practical experience, leaders struggle to understand what agile is all about. In this chapter we'll tell a detailed story that shows agile in action. We'll explain where the philosophy came from, and we'll outline the elements that make it such a different and more fruitful method of innovation.

Chapter 2: Scaling Agile. Scaling agile multiplies the degree of difficulty, but it can also produce exceptional results. Some organizations scale merely by adding more teams. Others pursue the goal of a truly agile enterprise, one that combines extensive use of agile teams with some bureaucratic functions, and that harmonizes the operations of both. This chapter introduces the remarkable transformation at Bosch, and it describes the steps a company must take as it creates an agile enterprise.

Chapter 3: How Agile Do You Want to Be? More agile is not always better agile. There is an optimal range of agility for every business, and for every activity within a business. But how to determine this range? Companies must find the right balance between stasis and chaos, and they must make the necessary trade-offs. They will need a new set of metrics that indicate how agile they are, how agile they want to become, whether they are moving in the right direction, and which constraints are impeding further progress. In this chapter, we'll show you how to address these issues using agile methods.

Chapter 4: Agile Leadership. Leading an agile enterprise, as Bosch executive Henk Becker discovered, isn't the same as leading a conventional company. Agile leaders spend less time reviewing the work of subordinates. They add value by adapting corporate strategies, leading critical agile teams, spending time with customers, mentoring individuals, and coaching teams. Changing one's own behaviors, restructuring daily routines, and developing new skills are far more challenging than telling others that they should do so, but they are also far more valuable. This chapter shows you how to go about it.

Chapter 5: Agile Planning, Budgeting, and Reviewing. Planning, budgeting, and reviewing systems are at the heart of command-and-control environments. Dell and other agile companies don't abolish these processes; they build agility into them. The companies conduct all three processes in frequent, adaptive cycles that rely extensively on bottom-up input. They prioritize strategic imperatives while welcoming unplanned initiatives. They regularly compare actual to expected performance to determine whether plans and budgets need changing.

Chapter 6: Agile Organization, Structures, and People Management. Companies are often tempted to copy an agile company's organization chart, thinking that new structures will make all the difference. But it doesn't work: you need more than structural change to break down silos and hierarchies. Agile enterprises often find themselves redesigning every element of their operating model—roles and decision rights, hiring and talent-management systems, and so on. Org charts may need to change as well. But deciding which tools to deploy, in what sequence, and to what degree requires considerable testing, learning, balancing, and customization—not copying.

Chapter 7: Agile Processes and Technology. Agile enterprises foster an obsession with customers, both internal and external. They aim to increase the quantity and quality of customer solutions. But customer solutions are only as good as the business processes that produce them, and those processes are frequently constrained by the technology that enables them. Some companies hesitate to even begin an agile transformation until their technology is ready to support it. But that can take years. Is this wise, or does it unnecessarily delay getting started?

Chapter 8: Doing Agile Right. The final chapter sums things up, proposing some rules for avoiding faddishness and describing the capabilities that have proven particularly important to success in scaling agile. We tell the inside story of Amazon, which created its own highly agile systems, tools, and ways of working, with results that have made it one of the world's most valuable companies. And we wind up the book with a short list of indispensable guidelines for creating agile enterprises and making yourself into an agile leader.

Throughout, we hope to show how an agile business delivers measurable improvements in outcomes—not only better financial performance but also greater customer loyalty, employee engagement, and societal benefits. That, of course, is the only valid objective of an agile transformation: improving performance and better achieving the enterprise's purpose. Agile isn't a goal in itself; it's a means to an end. Still, agile is about people as well as numbers. It's about creating an organization where talented people love coming to work, and where the bars of bureaucracy's iron cage are finally bent so that the human beings within can escape.

If you and your team are not having fun with agile, you're not doing it right.

A Note on the Research

Stories of agile teams are fun and persuasive, probably more persuasive than they should be. The problem is that stories are so easy to manipulate to make any point a pundit wants to make. (If you don't believe this, take a look at how differently CNN and Fox News report the exact same political stories.) Confirmation bias is a well-known challenge in digging for truth: human beings tend to look for and believe evidence that confirms what they want to hear. But is the story representative or a statistical aberration? How often has it occurred? How often have people done similar things but failed rather than succeeded?

We will use anecdotes about agile throughout this book, and we will do our best to report them fairly and insightfully. But we would like to put them in proper perspective. Agile is founded on empiricism and the scientific method. It stresses that hypotheses should be tested against real-world results rather than trusting alluring theories or intuitions. If agile works, there should be empirical data to put the anecdotes into a realistic statistical context. So, before diving further into *how* agile works, let's address the more fundamental issue of *whether* agile works.

Before writing this book, we dug up as much research as we could find on the results of agile approaches. We examined countless anecdotes, including those from hundreds of our own clients. We examined correlations from diagnostic surveys completed by thousands of agile practitioners who track their progress using our Bain Agility Quotient. To be as objective as possible, we also collected and analyzed seventy third-party research reports. (A complete list of the reports is included in appendix C so that you can peruse any or all of them.) They include journal articles, books, government papers, academic theses, conference papers, consultancy research, corporate research, and so on. Some reports have been updated regularly for many years. Others are metastudies synthesizing the findings of several researchers. Some are more academically rigorous than others. We probably missed some reports, which no doubt will annoy their proponents. For that, we apologize and promise to continue expanding and updating our database.

Overall, we were encouraged to find so much empirical data. We find significant evidence that agile approaches at the team, scale, and

FIGURE I-1

Number of research papers found addressing each question

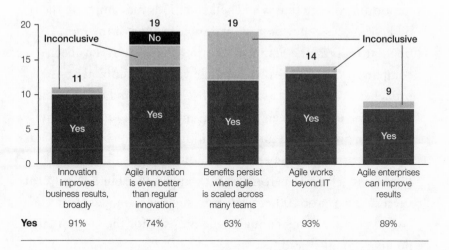

| Yes | 91% | 74% | 63% | 93% | 89% |

enterprise levels all improve results (figure I-1). Even without controlling for the quality of agile execution or throwing out inconve-
nient data points, we find little research suggesting that agile
approaches will, on average, hurt results. More specifically, we find
the following:

More innovation improves results. If you are disappointed in
your company's performance, feeling a little unbalanced, and
wondering whether to nudge the organization toward doing
less or more innovation, chances are good that the right answer
is more. Over 90 percent of the research reports we collected
show that innovation improves business results. None show
that it hurts. Apparently, few companies are doing so much innovation that it has reached the point of diminishing returns.
Some research suggests that stock prices may not reflect the
future benefits of innovation. But stock markets are famous for
their efficiency over time, not for their short-term accuracy.

Agile innovation is even better than traditional innovation. We
found twenty-one research reports on this topic. Three-fourths

of them found that agile is a superior way to do innovation, and only 10 percent concluded that agile did not help. It is important to note that while agile methods may improve the odds of success, they do not guarantee it. One of the most popular reports, the Standish Group's chaos study, has been comparing the success rates of agile versus traditional approaches in IT projects since 1994. These researchers now have a database of more than fifty thousand projects, and they find that agile projects are three-fifths more likely to succeed (42 percent versus 26 percent) and one-third as likely to fail (8 percent versus 21 percent). That's impressive, but a 42 percent success rate is not 100 percent, and such percentages matter only if you are doing enough agile projects for the laws of large numbers to take hold.[6]

Large-scale agile teams of teams also improve results. Despite concerns that agile was designed for individual teams and can't scale effectively, research shows otherwise. While large, complex problems have lower success rates using either traditional or agile approaches, agile's relative advantage over traditional approaches actually increases as complexity grows.

Agile innovation works in situations beyond IT. As we noted earlier, many people believe that agile began in IT and works only there. They are wrong on both counts. Agile began outside IT but rapidly gained traction in technology as the internet took off. Fourteen of fifteen research reports find that agile works effectively in a broad range of industries and functions within those industries.

Agile enterprises can improve results. Be aware that this is a less mature area of research. There are only nine reports at this writing, and few have yet been published in the most rigorous academic journals. Still, early results are encouraging. And as we compare agile mindsets and methods to a growing body of research on business results, employee engagement, and successful leaders and teams by academics (such as Teresa Amabile, Steven Kramer, Mary Shapiro, and MIT's Center for Collective Intelligence), consulting firms (including Gallup, Willis Towers Watson, and the Energy Project), and corporations (such as Google's Project Aristotle), we see remarkable consistency in the findings. Collectively, this substantial and growing body of research indicates that doing agile right is likely to help executives achieve their purposes and objectives.

And now, on to understanding more about what agile is and what it takes to create an agile enterprise.

1

HOW AGILE REALLY WORKS

I t's show time. Brian, the product owner of the Irresistible Snacks team, can't quite contain his excitement—though he notices, to his annoyance, that the excitement is tempered by periodic waves of anxiety. Engineers don't get anxious, he reminds himself. "The data is what it is. You just have to deal with it. This is just another project."

Sure it is. Brian's team is six weeks into its new-product development program. Today is its third sprint review, and team members will be asking twenty real-life customers to unwrap and sample the seven leading prototypes for the proposed new line of "healthy, indulgent" snack bars. Irresistible's executive committee will be out in full force to observe the session. Brian winces, remembering that several executive committee members openly opposed this new agile process from the beginning. Today is make or break. Maybe it shouldn't be, but it is.

Brian is a foodie by avocation and a food-development engineer by trade. But until recently he had always worked for small companies. Only two years ago, he was heading up new-product development for AlwaysAuthentic Nutrition, a rapidly growing young company that was beginning to reshape the snack shelves in supermarkets and convenience stores. An ideal job, he felt. On good days he could even bike to work from the Cleveland suburb where he lived.

But then came the news. Irresistible Snacks—a large processed-foods company that was part of an even bigger consumer-goods corporation—was acquiring AlwaysAuthentic. It was a generous offer. The smaller firm's owners made out like bandits, and a little of that large sum trickled out to the employees. But the acquisition brought layoffs, plant closures, and sad departures. What would come next? Brian had no false modesty about his reputation—he was known and respected throughout the industry—and he knew he could get a job pretty much anywhere. But where? And doing what? That was when one of Irresistible's top food engineers approached him. "You guys are fast on your feet," the engineer said to Brian. "You can teach us. We want to learn to innovate like a disruptive start-up. Join us. We need you."

It was a seductive idea, even for a small-company guy like Brian. Move up to the majors. Try out your skills on the big stage. The offer itself turned his head. The salary and benefits came to more than he had ever earned. There was the prospect of a bonus that would finally let him sock away some serious money.

So he had taken the plunge. And of course the job wasn't anything like what he expected. Budgets at Irresistible were tight. The company's procedures made it impossible to do anything without half a dozen signoffs, signoffs that required weeks to get. For a year and a half he felt as if he was perpetually running his head smack into the proverbial brick wall. Irresistible wanted to learn from the acquisition? Ha. More like they wanted to catch and kill a competitor, eliminating a threat to their old-school bureaucratic approach. After eighteen months of frustration, Brian was on the verge of quitting.

But then Irresistible's CEO, Lori, called Brian into her spacious corner office. Lori was blunt and to the point. "We've been losing market share for three years," she said. "This can't continue."

Brian was taken aback. For one thing, Lori was younger than he expected. He had seen her before, but only from a distance, and up close you could see that she was scarcely over forty. Quite a difference from the old guys who occupied the other executive suites. She was even younger than Brian, who at forty-nine was beginning to feel like a graybeard.

Nor did Lori mince words. "Our market research group has identified an opportunity in what we might call healthy but indulgent nutrition bars. Our product development group is telling me it will take at least twenty-four months to work up such a radical departure from our current products. Frankly, I don't think they really want it to succeed. They fear it will cannibalize our profitable lines of candy bars."

Lori leaned forward and looked straight at Brian. "I hear that you have a different attitude and a different way of doing things. I would like you to lead the development team for this new product line. What do you think?"

Wow. The scuttlebutt about Lori had been right: she was direct to the point of bluntness. He remembered hearing that her appointment had come as a surprise. She was a dynamite marketer, everybody agreed, but apparently some of the folks in Irresistible's C-suite had bridled at the board's decision to make her CEO.

Brian hesitated. Are you kidding? he thought. Aloud, he said, "I'm not sure I'm the right guy. Your organization has pretty much chewed me up and spit me out. But thanks for thinking of me." If she was going to be direct, he would be, too.

Lori laughed. "I expected that. I've heard you're getting a little fed up with this company. That's the problem right there." She came around the desk and sat down in the chair beside him. "Please, don't tell me no. Tell me what you need to succeed. If I can't give it to you, we'll shake hands and part ways on friendly terms."

Brian took a long evening to mull it over. He talked with his wife. He called a guy who had mentored him in the early years. The consensus was clear: What did he have to lose? Might as well give it a shot.

Three days later he was back in Lori's office, bustling with the kind of energy that had built his reputation in the business. "We'll need a multidisciplinary team. I'm proposing the following people: Danielle from product development, Jordan from packaging, Ellie from sales, Alyssa from marketing, Brianne from consumer insights, David from manufacturing, Gavin from supply chain, and Leah, who has experience coaching agile teams. I want 100 percent of all of them—no part timers. We'll need a space with lots of white boards where we can all work together face to face."

Brian looked at Lori to get her reaction. She nodded for him to go ahead.

"We'll need direct access to some innovative retail chains and also to potential consumers. The annual budgeting cycle just closed and we have no budget, so we'll need your help with funding. We can't waste time waiting in the back of the long line for help with safety, regulatory, legal, or IT assistance. If we can run this program like we used to run AlwaysAuthentic, we can release the best product on the market to select retail customers in six months rather than eighteen, with a full-scale rollout within twelve months instead of twenty-four. The clock will start as soon as the team is in place and we are ready to begin."

Lori looked a little surprised by the length and specificity of Brian's requests. "You sure there's nothing else?" she asked, allowing a small smile to cross her face.

Brian chuckled. "Just two more things. We need the executive committee to be involved. We'll welcome their ideas but not their traditional micromanagement methods. We get to decide what to do with their suggestions. And I don't want to sound disrespectful, but this will be especially important for the control freaks like Stacy, Kelly, and Eric to understand. If they start giving orders to their subordinates on our team, it won't work.

"And, finally"—might as well go for it all—"my real goal is to get every product development team, maybe every innovation team, to see the value of this approach and adopt it for themselves." He took a breath. "One or two product successes won't be enough to create the change we need. We don't just need a couple of agile teams, we need an agile enterprise."

For the first time, Lori balked. "Whoa," she said. "I agree we need some new products. I'm not sure we need a whole new system. Let's see how this project goes and then we can talk about where to go from there."

Brian realized he'd gotten a little carried away. "Fair enough," he said. "That's actually consistent with agile principles. But I'm going to take notes and share my observations with you along the way. The problem with this first pilot is that I know we can make it succeed. We can use your clout to bulldoze our way through almost anything, and we can create workarounds to systemic obstacles. I've seen this kind of coddling increase the odds of a team's success before. The problem is that it doesn't produce the learning environment or organizational changes necessary to scale dozens or hundreds of teams. Testing agile teams, just like testing any prototype, should reflect diverse, realistic conditions. We have to expose and fix the experiences that are causing the greatest frustrations with our current system. Will you at least promise to listen with an open mind?"

Lori found it easy to agree—what Brian was asking for was somewhere in the future, and anyway it all would depend on the results of the first team. What she was doing here was risky enough, but at least it was limited in time and scope. She would have to see what the future held.

"It's a deal," she said, and they shook hands.

Once outside Lori's office, Brian pulled out his notebook and turned to a blank page. He gave it a title and added a single bullet:

SCALING AGILE

- Agile teams versus an agile enterprise

The first three months were painful. Lori had to use all of her CEO authority to free up the right people. In the past, starting a new project was relatively easy. If you needed nine full-time equivalents, you'd put together a team with maybe four readily available people half time, ten with 25 percent allocations, and forty or fifty with 10 percent assignments. Functional leaders rarely objected—they didn't have to give up anyone, and having a representative on the project team would give them visibility into the effort. But this was crazy! Pulling nine good people full time out of their current operating roles? That was outrageous, and it wasn't going to happen without a fight. "How about taking Darrell instead? He has lots of time." "David doesn't want to do this agile stuff. He's afraid it will hurt his career." "Couldn't you do with 25 percent of Danielle? That's the way we've always done it. She's deep into that other key project and we don't have anyone to backfill for her. It will absolutely kill us to pull her off."

But Lori was firm, and pretty soon Brian had everyone he had asked for.

Brian wasn't demanding organizational superstars. He realized that if the team couldn't work with typical people, agile would never scale to dozens or hundreds of teams. But he refused to start until the team was properly established and fully committed. Along the way, he opened his notebook and started a new page with two bullets:

STRUCTURE AND PEOPLE

- Talent gaps

- Agile career paths

Once the team was in place, Brian wasted no time jumping into the work. Team members spent three days together. They learned agile mindsets and methods. They created a vision for their program. They reviewed the consumer insights work. They developed, prioritized, and sequenced a backlog of customer (retailer) and consumer (shopper) needs to address. They also decided that they would run in two-week sprints. This meant that every two weeks, they would

deliver a working version of some element of their program—a nutrition bar, a new wrapper, a manufacturing process, a marketing
program, sales materials, shelf displays, or any other element of the
end-to-end buying and using experience. For the first sprint, they
would build two versions of a new nutrition bar.

Danielle from product development took the lead. She reached
out to a chef who showed interest in the project, though he was
working on four other projects and had limited time. Brian opened
his notebook to the "Structure and People" heading and added a
sub-bullet under "Talent gaps."

STRUCTURE AND PEOPLE

- Talent gaps

  – Chefs

- Agile career paths

Alyssa from marketing wanted to create an online community of
two hundred consumers to get rapid feedback on prototypes. The
IT department told her they couldn't get to it for at least nine months.
Brian created a new page called "Processes and Technology" where
he added two bullets:

PROCESSES AND TECHNOLOGY

- Modular technology architecture (service-oriented architecture and microservices)

- Agile software development

He didn't like going outside for help, but he immediately con-
tracted with a third-party provider to create the online community
platform.

Next, Irresistible's food safety department said that nobody
would be allowed to taste any prototypes until the full range of

standard tests had been completed, which would take at least ten weeks. Brian couldn't understand that. The tests they were requiring went way beyond what federal regulators demanded for this type of product. Erin, the food safety manager, described some of the problems they had encountered in the past and explained why they had gone to one standardized system for all new products. Brian described how AlwaysAuthentic had developed four different testing and approval processes, customized to the amount of change required to existing products. In this case, he pointed out, they were not introducing any new ingredients, and there were no risky ingredients such as eggs that could carry salmonella. Erin said she would run that idea up the chain of command, but she wasn't optimistic that the higher-ups would change their minds. In the meantime, Brian proposed a couple of workarounds. "Could you please try to fast-track the approval process, and could we test samples with our team members and internal employees who sign consent forms?" Food safety checked with legal and agreed it would be OK.

Brian pulled out his notebook, turned to his "Processes and Technology" page, and entered another bullet:

PROCESSES AND TECHNOLOGY

- Modular technology architecture (service-oriented architecture and microservices)

- Agile software development

- Make business processes more agile

The team worked far too hard. But after two weeks, the members had their prototypes and were thrilled to present them. Sadly, CEO Lori and Kelly, the head of research and development, were the only people from the ten-member executive committee to show up for the review. Over the years, excomm members had learned that the first few reviews of any task force would only present future work plans, so they were a complete waste of time. They were wrong about this one. The team had prototypes to sample, based on inputs from the online consumer community. Lori tasted them, looked at the nutrition label mockup, and smiled broadly. "We never see new product prototypes in less than three months, and they often take six. You have done it in two weeks. They're certainly not perfect. The shapes are a little weird, and they are overbaked, but I can see where you're going." She paused. "And I like it."

The team was fired up, but Brian knew this was just the beginning. Members got together to review the first sprint and to consider changes in the backlog sequencing. They felt they needed more prototyping capacity. The consumer community had suggested five flavors that might be better than the two the team first chose. Producing that level of variety with enough volume for consumer sampling would require more than a test kitchen. They would soon need a pilot manufacturing line. David from manufacturing said there were no such testing lines—Irresistible had never needed them. He did find a small, seldom-used line that could be quickly converted, but it would cost about $250,000, maybe more. Brian quickly filed a capital request.

That led to an awkward conversation, worse than Brian had imagined. Colin, the CFO, was not known for his willingness to experiment, and he rejected the request out of hand. "Look, Brian, we're facing a tough year, and this is not in the budget. You'll have to find another way until we can work it into our next operating plan."

Brian was flabbergasted. "Of course it's not in the budget. Neither are the revenues that will come from it, nor the profits that will probably be fifty times higher than these costs. We can't wait that long."

Colin was not amused. "The costs are certain, but the revenues and profits are not. If everybody did what you're trying to do, this company would be in complete chaos. I have responsibilities to our shareholders, and to others in the company who are sticking to their budgets."

Brian pulled out his trump card. "I don't like doing this, but you know I'll need to talk to Lori about this, right?"

Colin shot back, "You do that!" and turned to some papers on his desk. Brian walked out and headed straight for Lori's office. Lori didn't like overruling her CFO, but she had promised to fund the project, so she did—quickly. Brian knew there would be additional budget requests, and he pulled out his notebook. He found a blank page and wrote:

PLANNING AND FUNDING

- More frequent and flexible planning and budgeting

The team continued pushing through barrier after barrier. Consumers wanted see-through packaging so they could see the actual product. The packaging department worried that clear packaging would shorten the products' shelf lives. Team members knew that start-up competitors had been using clear packaging for many months, so they found and quickly qualified a supplier that had solved the shelf life problem with new materials. Consumers also said they wanted some products with pistachios, cranberries, and higher cocoa content. Sourcing these materials required finding and qualifying new suppliers, and the new ingredients would also require more extensive safety testing. Brian and the team agreed that the extra time required for safety checks was well worth the delay. They restructured their activities to avoid running into those bottlenecks.

Gradually, word of the agile team's accomplishments spread. So did the number of people who wanted to get involved. Every member of the executive committee attended the second sprint to review five new prototypes. But it was just as Brian had feared: some of the more control-oriented executives began causing problems. They demanded make-up sessions for the reviews they had missed. They began issuing orders to their subordinates on the team. They insisted on updates prior to major reviews. The team members worried that failing to follow their bosses' orders could be disastrous for their careers. After all, when this program was over, they might be returning to their old jobs. Brian had no choice but to request time on the excomm's agenda to describe the agile process and clarify their roles in removing barriers rather than issuing orders.

Again, Lori reinforced Brian's message, and her personal prodding enabled temporary workarounds for most problems. Still, Brian continued to fill his notebook. Turning to a blank page, he created a category for "Leadership and Culture," adding several bullets:

LEADERSHIP AND CULTURE

- Trusting and empowering versus commanding and controlling

- Leaders operating as an agile team

- How managers view their value addition

- Removing impediments

The bullets under other categories grew as well. Under "Structure and People," he added three new bullets:

STRUCTURE AND PEOPLE

- Talent gaps

  - Chefs

- Agile career paths

- Performance management

- Positions, roles, and decision rights

- Clarify business definition and P&L ownership

Under "Processes and Technology," he continued adding bullets:

PROCESSES AND TECHNOLOGY

- Modular technology architecture (service-oriented architecture and microservices)

- Agile software development

- Make business processes more agile

- Break large, complex projects into smaller batches

- Focus all work on a customer need

The third sprint had the potential either to build momentum and commitment to agile processes or to give skeptical bureaucrats ammunition for killing it. Brian was taking another risk with the product review. Irresistible had always relied on third-party agencies to conduct product reviews. The rationale was sensible: they were skilled facilitators, plus they could be perfectly objective and nondefensive. But Brian wanted his team members to develop deep customer intimacy, and he didn't like waiting two or three weeks for the agency to deliver a polished report on the reviews. Few team members had ever done this sort of thing, and nearly all of them were nervous about how they would be judged by executive committee members.

Today, groups of five consumers each are filing into the four conference rooms surrounding the central observation room. The ten excomm members also congregate. Some focus their attention on only one group. Others rotate to hear the feedback from several groups. They talk among themselves about how to interpret the consumers' comments.

From the team members' perspectives, the reviews are successful. Four of the seven products tested have very high appeal to different consumer segments, and they receive good suggestions for ways to make the products even better. There are insights into packaging, labeling, marketing messages, and pricing. Three of the products have too many problems and fall to the bottom of the backlog. But what does the executive committee think? It's time to find out.

As the team members file into the central observation room, a few of the excomm members actually clap. "That was amazing," says Kelly, the R&D chief. "I have never seen so much progress after six weeks." Lori is more restrained, but she is clearly pleased—it looks as if the risk she took is paying off. All eyes turn to Colin, the CFO, his suit dark gray and his face dour. A small smile crosses his lips. "I think I can support this," he says.

From Colin, that is the equivalent of a four-star review, and it seems to open the floodgates. The executives shake hands with all the team members. They start asking what they can do to help. They even begin talking about other innovation projects that should adopt agile ways of working. Tomorrow will be the team's retrospective on what they can do better in the next sprint. But for tonight, it is time to celebrate—and for Brian to get some sleep.

Why Agile?

Irresistible Snacks, Brian, and the agile team he leads are of course fictitious. The story is a composite, based on hundreds of companies and teams that we have observed. But the fiction reflects two sets of facts about agile.

First: the *agile team* lies at the very heart of an agile enterprise. If you don't understand agile teams, you can't understand agile as an operating philosophy. That's why we described Irresistible's team in so much detail. In the rest of this chapter, we will examine where teams like Brian's came from. We'll describe in broader terms the principles and practices that govern what they do, how they work, and why they operate as they do. And we will of course define agile catchwords like *sprint* and *backlog*. But we first wanted to offer a sense of what these teams look and feel like, because both their origin and their operation reflect people's attempts to escape the confines of bureaucracy.

Second: it's easy enough to run a few agile teams in any organization. But if your ultimate goal is to scale agile, you need to begin changing the way people throughout the organization think and act. That's the significance of Brian's notebook. As you'll see, the challenges and obstacles he took note of are the challenges and obstacles that are likely to arise in any company that scales agile. These are the issues that we will take up in later chapters. We'll focus on what we think are the most important ones: leadership behaviors; planning, budgeting, and reviewing; organizational structures and people management; and processes and technology.

Roots of Agile

Some historians trace agile methodologies all the way back to Francis Bacon's articulation of the scientific method in 1620. In our view, a more reasonable starting point might be the 1930s, when the physicist and statistician Walter Shewhart of Bell Labs began applying continuous improvement cycles (specification-production-inspection) to products and processes. In 1938, W. Edwards Deming grew interested in Shewhart's work and popularized it with today's well-known plan-do-study-act (PDSA) cycle.

In 1986, Ikujiro Nonaka and coauthor Hirotaka Takeuchi published an article in *Harvard Business Review* called "The New New Product Development Game."[1] Studying manufacturers that were releasing successful innovations far faster than competitors, the authors identified a team-oriented method that had changed the design and development process for products such as Fuji-Xerox's copiers, Honda's automobile engines, and Canon's cameras. Rather than following conventional relay race methods of product development— one group of functional specialists handing off its completed phase to the next functional stage—these companies were using what Takeuchi and Nonaka called a "rugby" approach, "where a team tries to go the whole distance as a unit, passing the ball back and forth."[2]

In 1993, Jeff Sutherland faced what seemed like an impossible task. Easel Corporation, a software company, needed to develop a new product to replace its legacy offerings in less than six months. Sutherland already had a strong background in methodologies such as rapid application development, object-oriented design, PDSA cycles, and skunkworks. He hoped to create a skunkworks-like culture in the middle of Easel's corporate headquarters, blending the benefits of both separation and integration. So he began by learning everything he could about maximizing organizational productivity. Reading hundreds of papers and interviewing leading product-management experts, he found himself intrigued by several provocative ideas.

One came from a Bell Labs article on the Borland Quattro Pro team, suggesting that short daily team meetings increased group productivity dramatically.[3] Similar tips turned up in other materials. But the capstone concept for Sutherland was the discovery of Takeuchi and Nonaka's rugby approach, even though it focused on manufacturing rather than software. Borrowing many of their article's key ideas and filling in specific operational practices, Sutherland created a new way of developing software; honoring the rugby imagery, he dubbed his approach *Scrum*. Scrum methods enabled him to finish his seemingly impossible project on time, under budget, and with fewer bugs than any previous release. He then collaborated with longtime colleague Ken Schwaber to codify the approach, and in 1995 the pair presented Scrum to the public for the first time.

Of course, Sutherland and Schwaber weren't alone in their search for innovative methods. The information age was exploding. Disruptive technologies were terrorizing slow-footed competitors. Start-ups and incumbents alike were seeking better ways to adapt to the unfamiliar and turbulent environment. Software was becoming an integral part of nearly every business function, and many creative software developers were working hard on better methods of programming to increase adaptability.

In 2001, seventeen developers who called themselves *organizational anarchists* met in Snowbird, Utah, to share their ideas. Sutherland and other proponents of Scrum were among them. The group also included advocates of several competitive approaches, including Extreme Programming (XP), Crystal, Adaptive Software Development (ASD), Feature-Driven Development (FDD), and the Dynamic Systems Development Method (DSDM). All these approaches were collectively known as lightweight frameworks because they used fewer, simpler rules to allow faster adaptation to rapidly changing environments. (Not many of the attendees found the lightweight terminology flattering.)

A New Name

Although they disagreed on much, members of the group eventually settled on a new name for the movement: agile. The word was suggested by an attendee who had been reading the book *Agile Competitors and Virtual Organizations: Strategies for Enriching the Customer*, by Steven L. Goldman, Roger N. Nagel, and Kenneth Preiss.[4] The book offered one hundred examples of companies—including ABB, Federal Express, Boeing, Bose, and Harley-Davidson—that were developing new ways of adapting to turbulent markets. Name in hand, attendees then forged consensus on a call to arms, which they dubbed the Manifesto for Agile Software Development. The manifesto spelled out four key values that everyone agreed on— such things as "working software over comprehensive documentation" and "responding to change over following a plan." Later in the meeting, and continuing over the next few months, they developed twelve operating principles, such as "Our highest priority is to satisfy the customer through early and continuous delivery of valuable software" and "Simplicity—the art of maximizing the amount of work not done—is essential."[5] From 2001 on, all development frameworks that aligned with these values and principles would be known as agile techniques.

Once the Snowbird meeting had canonized a creed for agile innovation, the agile movement spread rapidly. The signatories posted their document online and invited others to add their names as supporters. Most members of the original group, joined by a number of new adherents, reconvened later in the year to discuss ways to disseminate agile principles. All agreed to write and speak on the topic.

Over time, the use of agile grew. In 2016, one of this book's authors (Darrell Rigby) joined Sutherland and Takeuchi to write a *Harvard Business Review* article called "Embracing Agile."[6] By then, the article reported, National Public Radio was employing agile methods to create new programming, John Deere to develop some of its new machines, and Saab to produce the Gripen jet. Mission Bell Winery, in California, was using the methods "for everything from wine production to warehousing to running its senior leadership group."[7] OpenView Venture Partners, based in Massachusetts, was encouraging its portfolio companies to adopt them. Agile has spread further since then, as the examples in this book will show. While its complex family tree sometimes provokes passionate debate among agile practitioners, two things are clear from this brief history. First, agile's roots and applications extend far beyond its uses in information technology; they are relevant to many different elements of an organization. Second, agile is likely to continue to spread. It was developed to help people escape the clutches of bureaucracy—and what the Irresistible Snacks of the world need now, more than anything else, is the ability to restore the balance between bureaucracy and innovation.

How Agile Teams Operate

Agile teams work differently from chain-of-command bureaucracies. They are best suited to innovation—that is, the profitable application of creativity to improve customer solutions, business processes, and technology.

To tackle an opportunity, the organization forms and empowers a small team, usually three to nine people, most of whom are assigned full time. The team is multidisciplinary and includes all the skills necessary to complete its tasks. It manages itself and is strictly accountable for every aspect of the work. Senior leaders tell team members where to innovate but not how. Confronted with a large, complex problem, the team breaks it into modules, develops solutions to each component through rapid prototyping and tight feedback loops, and integrates the solutions into a coherent whole. Members place more value on adapting to change than on sticking to a plan. They hold themselves accountable for outcomes (such as growth, profitability, and customer loyalty), not just outputs (such as lines of code or number of new products). The teams work closely with customers, both external and internal. Ideally, this puts responsibility for innovation in the hands of the people who are closest to those customers. It reduces layers of control and approval, thereby speeding up work and increasing the teams' motivation.

Agile approaches are a combination of both mindsets and methods. Although religious wars break out among zealots battling over which is more important, the debate is absurd. Is your head or your heart more important to survival? You die unless you have both. As a philosophy, agile focuses intently on customers. Practitioners believe that every work activity has a customer, and that work should be structured around meeting customers' needs as effectively and profitably as possible. The finance group, for instance, serves the operating units it funds, and they should provide feedback on their satisfaction with finance. Agile teams thus have backlogs—

essentially, prioritized and sequenced to-do lists—based on customer needs, not tasks to complete.

The agile mindset abhors work in process (WIP). WIP ties up work while adding no value. The longer it sits, the more it costs. Meanwhile, customer needs are changing, competitors are innovating, and WIP is growing obsolete. So agile favors small batches, produced in time-limited (less than a month) work cycles called sprints. Contrary to some skeptics' opinions, agile practitioners do not run short sprints to make team members work harder. They run short sprints to encourage fast feedback from real customers. A short sprint encourages agile teams to think about how they can quickly create something worth testing. Short sprints also make it easier for team members to synchronize long, slow processes with fast ones.

The team's initiative owner, also known as a product owner, is ultimately responsible for delivering value to customers (including internal customers and future users) and to the business. The person in this role usually comes from a business function and divides his or her time between working with the team and coordinating with key stakeholders: customers, senior executives, and business managers. The initiative owner may use a technique such as design thinking or crowdsourcing to build a comprehensive portfolio backlog of promising opportunities. Then he or she continually and ruthlessly rank-orders that list according to the latest estimates of value to internal or external customers and to the company. The initiative owner doesn't tell the team who should do what or how long tasks will take. Rather, team members themselves create a simple road map and plan in detail only those activities that won't change before execution. They break the highest-ranked tasks into small modules, decide how much work they will take on and how to accomplish it, develop a clear definition of *done*, and then start building working versions of the product in sprints. A process facilitator (often a trained scrum master) guides the process. This person protects the team from distractions and helps it put its collective intelligence to work.

The process is wholly transparent. Team members hold brief daily coordination meetings to review progress and identify roadblocks. They resolve disagreements through experimentation and feedback rather than through endless debates or appeals to authority. They test small working prototypes of part or all of the offering with a few customers for short periods of time. If customers get excited, a prototype may be released immediately, even if some senior executive isn't a fan or others think it needs more bells and whistles. The team then brainstorms ways to improve future cycles and prepares to attack the next top priority.

Compared with traditional management approaches, agile offers a number of major benefits, all of which have been studied and documented. It increases team productivity and employee satisfaction. It minimizes the waste inherent in redundant meetings, repetitive planning, excessive documentation, quality defects, and low-value product features. By improving visibility and continually adapting to customers' changing priorities, agile improves customer engagement and satisfaction, brings the most valuable products and features to market faster and more predictably, and reduces risk. By engaging team members from multiple disciplines as collaborative peers, it broadens organizational experience and builds mutual trust and respect. Finally, by dramatically reducing the time squandered on micromanaging functional projects, it allows senior managers to devote themselves more fully to higher-value work that only they can do: creating and adjusting the corporate vision; prioritizing strategic initiatives; simplifying and focusing work; assigning the right people to tasks; increasing cross-functional collaboration; and removing impediments to progress.

Agile practitioners are extraordinarily skeptical of managers' abilities to predict, command, and control innovative solutions, especially when what to deliver and how to deliver it are vague. As a thought experiment, imagine that you are charged with designing an autonomous vehicle to drive from Minnesota to Florida. You would have two options:

The first is to develop a deterministic model for the vehicle. You could study every detail of the roads between Minnesota and Florida, predicting every possible twist and turn, traffic light change, pedestrian or deer crossing the road, traffic accident, and weather condition. When the car crashes during a trial run (as it inevitably must), you will be told to work harder and to improve your predictive skills. But the chances are slim that more work will solve the problem. If the vehicle were traveling inside a tube, maybe the predict-and-plan model would work. In the real world, things get very complicated very quickly.

A different approach is to program the vehicle to adapt to changing conditions. Start by determining why someone might want to go from Minnesota to Florida in the first place. If hurricane conditions make Florida too dangerous, consider rerouting to California. Then anticipate the situations that could arise, develop ways to measure those situations, create sensors to track them, and incorporate appropriate responses to deal with them. Collect data from weather centers, traffic monitors, and other drivers. Provide the data to those same sensors from your vehicle. "I am approaching this intersection, be sure to stop for the light." If the feedback loops are short enough and sensitive enough, the transitions will be smooth and comfortable rather than abrupt and jarring. That's what agile is all about— learning as you go.

FIVE KEY TAKEAWAYS

1. The agile team is the heart of the agile approach. If you don't understand how an agile team works, you will struggle to scale agile across an entire business.

2. Agile teams believe that customer feedback is better than management hunches for determining which innovation efforts are most important and how best to adapt them.

3. Agile teams do not use sprints to make people work harder or faster. They use sprints to get faster feedback from real customers (external or internal) about what those customers truly value.

4. Bureaucrats will fear giving up control until they allow controlled experiments and find that success rates triple—and that customers, employees, and shareholders are all happier.

5. Trying to predict, command, and control innovation when what to deliver and how to deliver it are vague and unpredictable is foolhardy.

SCALING AGILE

Saab's aeronautics business has more than one hundred agile teams operating across software, hardware, and fuselage for its Gripen fighter jet, a $43 million product that is daunting in its complexity. At 7:30 a.m. each front-line team holds a fifteen-minute meeting to flag impediments, some of which cannot be resolved within that team. At 7:45 the impediments requiring coordination are escalated to a team of teams, where leaders work to either settle or further escalate issues. This approach continues, and by 8:45 the executive action team has a list of the critical issues it must resolve to keep progress on track. Saab Aeronautics also coordinates its teams through a common rhythm of three-week sprints, a project master plan that is treated as a living document, and the colocation of traditionally disparate parts of the organization—for instance, putting test pilots and simulators with development teams. As we noted earlier, the product that emerges from all this has been deemed the world's most cost-effective military aircraft.

SAP SE, the enterprise software company, was an early scaler of agile, launching the process a decade ago. Its leaders expanded agile first in its software development units—a highly customer-focused segment where they could test and refine the approach. They established a small consulting group to train, coach, and embed the new way of working, and they created a results tracker so that everyone could see the teams' gains. "Showing concrete examples of impressive productivity gains from agile created more and more pull from the organization," said Sebastian Wagner, who was then a consulting manager in that group.[1] Over the next two years, the company rolled out agile to more than 80 percent of its development organizations, creating more than two thousand teams. People in sales and marketing saw the need to adapt in order to keep up, so those areas went next. Once the front end of the business was moving at speed, it was time for the back end to make the leap, so SAP shifted its group working on internal IT systems to agile.

USAA has several hundred agile teams up and running at this writing and plans to continue adding them. The company—a financial services firm specializing in serving American military personnel—ties the activities of agile teams to the people responsible for business units and product lines. The goal is to ensure that managers responsible for specific parts of the profit and loss statement (P&L) understand how cross-functional teams will influence their results. The company has senior leaders who act as general managers in each line of business and are fully accountable for business results. But those leaders rely on member-focused, cross-organizational teams to get much of the work done. USAA also depends on technology and digital resources assigned to the experience owners; the goal here is to ensure that business leaders have the end-to-end resources to deliver the outcomes they have committed to.

Over the past decade, leaders who experienced or heard about agile teams began asking some compelling questions. What if a company were to launch dozens, hundreds, or even thousands of agile teams throughout the organization? Could whole segments of the business learn to operate in this manner? Would scaling agile improve corporate performance as much as agile methods improve individual team performance? Companies as diverse as 3M, Amazon, Bosch, Dell, Facebook, Google, Haier, ING, Lego, Microsoft, Netflix, PayPal, Royal Bank of Scotland, Riot Games, Salesforce, Spotify, and Target have all increased the scale and scope of their agile teams. We have worked with and studied many such enterprises. Though their results are generally impressive, the differences in companies' approaches, outcomes, and even definitions of scaling agile are striking.

What Does It Mean to Scale Agile?

One definition of scaling agile is simple: add more agile teams. Increase their number to fifty, one hundred, or more. Widen the scope of agile, so that teams are functioning in several different parts of the organization. Learn to use teams of teams to tackle very large projects. We have seen many different examples of this kind of scaling, and most commentary about scaled agile focuses on it. We refer to this as *agile at scale*, and it describes the experience so far of the typical large organization.

But there is another definition of scaling agile, which for most companies is still on the horizon. We call it creating the *agile enterprise*, and in some ways that's what this book is about. Agile at scale focuses on improving the performance of agile teams while allowing bureaucracy and innovation efforts to coexist. Agile enterprises, in contrast, focus on creating agile business systems: they transform bureaucracy and innovation efforts into symbiotic partners that collaborate to deliver better results. The chapters that follow will discuss in detail the question of how far and how fast to proceed, along with the many changes in behavior, processes, and operations that are required to create an agile enterprise. In those chapters we'll try to cover everything from reshaping IT and changing the budget process to revamping the company's talent management and compensation system. In this chapter we have a more modest but equally important objective. We want to provide an overview of what's involved in creating an agile enterprise and contrast it to the more modest ambition of doing agile at scale. We also want to examine why a company might want to embark on such an ambitious and sometimes perilous journey.

Agile at Scale

A company that pursues agile at scale is likely to remain bureaucratic in its fundamental approach to business. Typically, the customer the company is aiming to satisfy is the shareholder. The primary objective is to launch enough agile teams to improve financial results. To ensure that the program is profitable, management may combine cost-cutting measures, including layoffs, with support for more agile teams. A program management office typically drives the transformation, just as previous task forces drove other transformation initiatives. The program office's job is to change people's behaviors—installing agile teams, promoting the supporters, and fixing or firing people who actively resist the transformation. Typically, too, the executive team takes responsibility for keeping agile teams on track and on budget. After a couple of years, there will be many more agile teams, and these teams will likely coordinate among themselves quite effectively. Yet they will almost certainly be working within a bureaucratic system of corporate management, operations, support, and control—a system that runs pretty much as it has for decades.

Earlier, we identified some of these practices as pitfalls to avoid—and they are, if you want to create a true agile enterprise. But agile at scale doesn't always go disastrously wrong, and for some companies it may be the right choice. Adding dozens of agile teams is manageable within traditional governance processes, and creative workarounds can overcome most obstacles. Senior executives can control the work of a few dozen agile teams without destroying the teams' performance or morale. Since agile teams almost always per-form better than traditional project teams, team results usually improve. Still, there are serious risks to this approach. Over time, nonagile parts of the organization may escalate their complaints. People in these units may feel that agile teams are stealing the best people, pilfering money that could be used in their own functions, disregarding budgeting procedures, endangering good management practices, and in general putting the company at risk. The resultant discord may force the organization to retreat to more conventional ways of doing things, sacrificing whatever gains have been made. There is an opportunity cost as well: a company that limits itself to agile at scale gives up the potential gains of creating an agile enterprise.

But the most difficult problem—and one that is likely to be coun-terintuitive—is this: even though agile teams may develop innova-tions better and faster than ever before, leaders are likely to find that the company's overall innovation velocity is not improving. When they investigate that problem, they uncover the concept of flow efficiency.

The time it takes an agile team to release an innovation is deter-mined by two factors, the time required to work on the innovation and the time spent waiting on others. Waiting times include delays caused by operating processes such as strategic planning calendars, decision approval processes, budgeting and funding cycles, software release schedules, legal or regulatory constraints, people allocation processes, and dozens of other factors. A company's flow efficiency is calculated by dividing work time by the sum of work time plus wait time (see figure 2-1). Empirical data shows that the flow effi-ciency for most companies is seldom better than 15 or 20 percent. So even if the speed of agile work improves by one-fifth, the enter-prise's overall innovation velocity could improve by only 3 or 4 percent. That's a barely noticeable difference. Moreover, when companies fire operating and support people to pay for agile teams without reinventing business processes, it leaves fewer people to do

FIGURE 2-1

Flow efficiency is seldom better than 15–20 percent for most companies

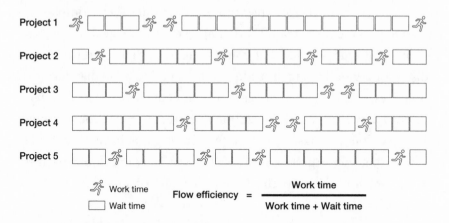

Flow efficiency = $\dfrac{\text{Work time}}{\text{Work time} + \text{Wait time}}$

Data source: Daniel Vacanti, author of *Actionable Agile Metrics for Predictability: An Introduction*, and David J. Anderson, coauthor of *Kanban Maturity Model: Evolving Fit-for-Purpose Organizations*.

the same amount of work. That leads to slower speeds, longer queues, longer waits, and more work in process. To make matters worse, managers are likely to be desperate for ways to improve utilization and reduce cost, so they fill the wait time by giving people additional projects. This leads to multitasking, which increases switching costs, reduces productivity, exacerbates wait times, and further slows development cycles. In the end, the speed of innovation can actually decline.

Here's a telling example, and a real-world counterpart to the Irresistible Snacks' experience. A large financial services company we examined launched a pilot to build its next mobile app using agile methodologies. Of course, the first step was to assemble a team. That required a budget request to authorize and fund the project. The request went into the batch of submissions vying for approval in the next annual planning process. After months of reviews, the company finally approved funding. The pilot produced an effective app that customers praised, and the team was proud of its work. But before the app was released, it had to pass vulnerability testing in a traditional waterfall process (a protracted sequence in which the computer code is tested for documentation, functionality, efficiency, and standardization), and the queue for the process was long. Then the app had to be integrated into core IT systems—which involved another waterfall process with a six-to-nine-month logjam. In the end, the total time to release improved very little.

So how do we deal with such serious challenges? That's the purpose of an agile enterprise.

The Agile Enterprise

Agile enterprises are more than aggregations of teams. They are carefully balanced operating models that use agile methods to (1) run the business reliably and efficiently, (2) change the business to capitalize on unpredictable opportunities, and (3) harmonize the two activities. So executives aiming to create such an enterprise approach the scaling process with a different mindset. They do not try to separate agile teams from the rest of the organization as if the two groups were enemies. Nor do they try to put every employee into an agile team. Although agile innovation teams are an essential element of an agile enterprise, they usually involve only 10 to 50 percent of employees. Most of the work and most of the people in agile systems focus on running the business—operations, support, and control functions.

In an agile enterprise, moreover, leaders view the scaling process itself as an agile initiative—in fact, as the most vital of all agile initiatives. Senior executives manage the transition as an agile team. They understand that such transitions are continuous improvement products, not projects with predictable end points or fixed completion dates. They do not view employees as subordinates and change resisters but as customers whose engagement and feedback will be critical to success. The executive team sets priorities and sequences opportunities to improve those customers' experiences and increase their satisfaction. Leaders plunge in to solve problems and remove constraints rather than delegate that work to subordinates.

Bosch, a leading global supplier of technology and services with more than 400,000 associates and operations in sixty-plus countries, took this approach. As leaders began to see that traditional top-down management was no longer effective in a fast-moving, globalized world, the company became an early adopter of agile methods. But different business areas seemed to require different approaches, and Bosch's first attempt to scale agile unintentionally led to a divisive culture—one in which hot new businesses were run with agile teams while traditional functions were left out of the action, compromising the goal of a holistic transformation. In 2015 members of the board of management, led by CEO Volkmar Denner, decided to build a more unified approach to agile teams. The board acted as a steering committee and named Felix Hieronymi, a software engineer turned agile expert, to guide the effort.

At first Hieronymi expected to manage the assignment the same way Bosch managed most projects: with a goal, a target completion date, and regular status reports to the board. But that approach felt inconsistent with agile principles, and the company's divisions were just too skeptical of yet another centrally organized program. So the team shifted gears. "The steering committee turned into a working committee," Hieronymi told us. "The discussions got far more interactive." The team compiled and rank-ordered a backlog of corporate priorities that was regularly updated, and it focused on steadily removing companywide barriers to greater agility. Members fanned out to engage division leaders in dialogue. "Strategy evolved from an annual project to a continuous process," Hieronymi said. "The members of the management board divided themselves into small agile teams and tested various approaches—some with a 'product owner' and an 'agile master'—to tackle tough problems or work on fundamental topics. One group, for instance, drafted the ten new leadership principles released in 2016. They personally experienced the satisfaction of increasing speed and effectiveness. You can't gain this experience by reading a book." Today Bosch operates with a mix of agile teams and traditionally structured units. But it reports that nearly all areas have adopted agile values, are collaborating more effectively, and are adapting more quickly to increasingly dynamic marketplaces. (We'll have more on Bosch in the following chapters.)

Building an agile enterprise does *not* mean doing away with bureaucracy completely. Anyone contemplating it has to pass F. Scott Fitzgerald's famous test of a first-rate intelligence: "the ability to hold two opposed ideas in the mind at the same time and still retain the ability to function."[2] Indeed, the organization itself needs that kind of intelligence.

On the one hand, an agile enterprise needs agile teams pursuing innovation all over the place—and by innovation, we do not mean simply the introduction of new products such as Irresistible's proposed line of snacks. Companies need innovation in business processes, in technology, in human resources, even in finance. Agile teams could take hard looks at supply-chain procedures, HR policies, and customer-service practices.

In short, an agile enterprise is a cross-functional team. The leaders of an agile enterprise must run the business reliably and efficiently, change the business to capitalize on unpredictable opportunities, and harmonize the two activities. This view is consistent with the Chinese philosophy of duality, or yin and yang. Operations and innovations are complementary and interdependent activities that need each other to succeed. The tensions, checks, and balances are features of, not flaws in, a healthy operating system (figure 2-2). That's why we stress the idea of balance throughout this book. Of course, the right balance will vary by industry, company, and activity within a business. Managing R&D activities for an innovation leader in robotics will demand far more change than managing mining operations for a commodity player in the gravel industry.

FIGURE 2-2

The yin and yang of business

Change the
business
(innovation)

Run the
business
(operations)

Creating an Agile Vision and Strategy

Leaders aiming for agile enterprises know that a vision of the future
can help to break through constraining bureaucratic mindsets. They
know that an effective strategy and the priorities it imposes are essential for focusing agile teams on the right initiatives. But they also
know that forecasts of the future are usually wrong, and they probably aren't certain how far or how fast they want to proceed. (Chapter 3 examines this subject in detail.) So how can they develop and
sell a vision and a strategy for achieving it without looking foolish
when either or both prove to be flawed? Sadly, the most common
approach is to refuse to recognize and admit such shortcomings—
though replacement leaders are delighted to point them out as they
step in to change course.

A better way is to think like an agile team and to create a vision
in just that manner.

This process begins with the only reason any agile team exists at
all: to improve performance by helping some group of customers
progress toward their goals. Agile teams typically express those customer goals in the form of user stories. The simplest user stories

FIGURE 2-3

Simple user stories

As a: _____(type of customer)_____

I want: _____(desired solutions and experiences)_____

So that: _____(customer goals; functional and emotional benefits)_____

look something like figure 2-3. More sophisticated versions look more like figure 2-4.

With appropriate user stories in place, leaders can then explore the world through the eyes of various customers of an agile enterprise, including end-use consumers, operations employees, innovation employees, financial investors, and the external community. Here is another place where balance is essential. Over the past few decades, corporate weighting of short-term financial results has

FIGURE 2-4

More sophisticated user stories

As a: _____(type of customer)_____

Struggling to: _____(customer goals)_____

While: _____(specific episode of the customer journey)_____

I am frustrated by: _____(challenges and obstacles)_____

And often cope by: _____(unsatisfactory workarounds)_____

I would love: _____(desired experiences and definition of quality)_____

So that I can: _____(desired functional and emotional benefits)_____

If you solve this, I would give up: _____(competing alternatives)_____

Though I fear I would lose: _____(benefits of alternatives)_____

And I worry that your solution might: _____(perceived risks and adoption anxieties)_____

grown to unhealthy levels (and planning to achieve top quartile total shareholder returns, as so many management teams do, is guaranteed to fail at 75 percent of companies anyway). It has therefore become fashionable for agile gurus to throw financial results on the scrap heap along with bureaucracy, and to recommend focusing only on customer satisfaction. No doubt that makes for a newsworthy soundbite. But unless you're going to give your products away for free and then close up shop, you have to balance customer satisfaction with other objectives.

The first step, then, is to develop a strategic hypothesis that can effectively balance and integrate customer solutions to build a sustainable enterprise. The next step is to show some humility. Admit that parts of the strategic hypothesis may need to adapt. This requires more than shrugging shoulders, throwing hands in the air, and declaring, "We have no clue if this will work, but it sure would be cool if it did!" Instead, leaders can describe the potential benefits of the strategy, identify the assumptions that must hold true for the strategy to succeed, and then create a prioritized and sequenced list of activities that move the organization toward that vision while testing assumptions and adapting along the way. We call this sequenced list of activities an enterprise backlog, and it is built jointly with a taxonomy of teams.

A Taxonomy of Teams

Just as agile teams compile a backlog of work to be accomplished in the future, companies that successfully scale up agile usually begin by creating an enterprise backlog and a taxonomy of teams required to achieve it. The taxonomy identifies key customer solutions and the business processes and technology that support them. It then determines where to deploy teams and how to coordinate or combine the teams with critical interdependencies. The first step identifies all the experiences that could significantly affect external and internal customer decisions, behaviors, and satisfaction. These can usually be divided into a dozen or so major experiences. For example, one of a retail customer's major experiences is to buy and pay for a product, which in turn can be divided into dozens of more specific experiences (the customer may need to choose a payment method, use a coupon, redeem loyalty points, complete the checkout process, and get a receipt). The second step examines the relationships among these customer experiences and key business processes (improved checkout procedures to reduce time in lines, for instance), aiming to reduce overlapping responsibilities and increase collaboration between process teams and customer experience teams. The third focuses on developing technology systems (such as better mobile-checkout apps) to improve the business processes that will support customer experience teams.

The taxonomy of a $10 billion business might identify anywhere from 250 to 1,000 or more potential teams. Those numbers sound daunting, and senior executives are often loath even to consider so much change ("How about if we try two or three of these things and see how it goes?"). But the value of a taxonomy is that it encourages exploration of a transformational vision while breaking the journey into small steps that can be paused, turned, or halted at any time. It also helps leaders spot constraints. Once you've identified the teams you could launch and the sorts of people you would need to staff them, for instance, you need to ask: Do we have those people? If so, where are they? A taxonomy reveals your talent gaps and the kinds of people you must hire or retrain to fill them. Leaders can also see how each potential team fits into the goal of delivering better customer experiences.

USAA's taxonomy, for instance, is fully visible to everyone across the enterprise. "If you don't have a really good taxonomy, you get redundancy and duplication," then-COO Carl Liebert told us when we were researching this book. "I want to walk into an auditorium and ask, 'Who owns the member's change-of-address experience?' And I want a clear and confident response from a team that owns that experience, whether a member is calling us, logging into our website on a laptop, or using our mobile app. No finger-pointing. No answers that begin with 'It's complicated.'" The intent of USAA's taxonomy is to clarify how to engage the right people in the right work without creating confusion. This kind of link is especially important when hierarchical organizational structures do not align with customer behaviors. For example, many companies have separate structures and P&Ls for online and offline operations—but customers want seamlessly integrated omnichannel experiences. A clear taxonomy that launches the right cross-organizational teams makes such alignment possible.

Wait, you may be thinking, how am I supposed to pay for all these teams? The answer, in most cases, is by curtailing unproductive innovation activities and reconfiguring continuing innovation initiatives as agile teams. Often, a taxonomy will reveal that about one-third of current innovation teams are working on things that customers don't want or teams can't deliver. Previous processes didn't have any good way of putting a stop to these activities other than waiting until they ran out of budget. Agile changes that. For teams that continue, agile methods should increase productivity by at least 20 percent, sometimes substantially more. As agile teams move on to redesigning business processes and technology, further efficiencies will emerge.

Sequencing the Transition

Taxonomy in hand, the leadership team sets priorities and sequences initiatives. Leaders must consider multiple criteria, including strategic importance, budget limitations, availability of people, return on investment, cost of delays, risk levels, and interdependencies among teams. The most important—and the most frequently overlooked—are the pain points felt by customers and employees on the one hand and the organization's capabilities and constraints on the other. These determine the right balance between how fast the rollout should proceed and how many teams the organization can handle simultaneously.

A few companies, facing urgent strategic threats and in need of radical change, have pursued big-bang, everything-at-once deployments in some units. One such was ING, which we mentioned in the book's introduction. Bart Schlatmann, the chief operating officer at the time, reflected on the experience in an interview:

> I still remember January of 2015 when we announced that all employees at headquarters were put on "mobility," effectively meaning they were without a job. We requested everyone to reapply for a position in the new organization. This selection process was intense, with a higher weighting for culture and mindsets than knowledge or experience. We chose each of the 2,500 employees in our organization as it is today—and nearly 40 percent are in a different position to the job they were in previously. Of course, we lost a lot of people who had good knowledge but lacked the right mindset; but knowledge can be easily regained if people have the intrinsic capability.[3]

He is understandably putting a favorable gloss on the experience. But can you imagine the terror and trauma the initiative must have provoked in the workforce? Why start with such a risky and costly move? Such an approach emphasizes cost savings more than innovation and growth. Fostering a new way of working with people who have been fearing for their jobs—and 40 percent of whom are in new roles—gets the whole project off to a rocky beginning. And that's not to mention the fact that the leadership team just role-modeled the exact opposite of agile values in doing so.

The fact is, big-bang transitions are hard. They require total leadership commitment, a receptive culture, enough talented and experienced agile practitioners to staff hundreds of teams without depleting other capabilities, and highly prescriptive instruction manuals to align everyone's approach. They also require a high tolerance of risk, along with contingency plans to deal with unexpected breakdowns. Companies short on those assets are better off rolling out agile in sequenced steps, with each unit matching the implementation of opportunities to its capabilities. With a vision sketch and sequenced backlog, senior executives can launch an initial wave of agile teams, gather data on the value those teams create and the constraints they face, and then decide whether, when, and how to take the next step. Again, we'll discuss the how-far-and-how-fast issue in more detail in chapter 3.

Planning for Interdependencies

One of the features of agile is that it breaks complex problems into smaller, more manageable modules. That's one reason an agile enterprise needs so many agile teams. But coordinating and integrating those modules then becomes a central task. It requires complete transparency among teams, so that each knows what the others are doing and what the effects are likely to be. In bureaucracies, everything flows back to a central hub for direction and approvals. An agile enterprise, by contrast, must develop a network with nodes that can work with each other without a central hub. That's why transparency is essential. Technology systems can help, but regular face-to-face communications are often necessary.

Sometimes a small program management office can also be helpful, both with coordination and as a supplement to the executive committee. But remember that the goal is an agile enterprise. A program or transformation office cannot become the agile police or get between leaders and their teams. It has to stay lean and service-oriented, watching the results of the agile teams and bringing improvement opportunities to the executive team. If the transition is as important as we say it is, the executive committee should devote substantial time to it, just as at Bosch. The program office can also be supplemented by a center of excellence related to agile, focused primarily on training and coaching agile teams. The trainers and coaches can be available to all, but they should be called in only at the request of teams that want their services.

When launching the transition, too many companies make the mistake of going for easy wins. They put teams into offsite incubators. They intervene to create easy workarounds to systemic obstacles. Such coddling increases the odds of a team's success, but it doesn't produce the learning environment or organizational changes necessary to scale dozens or hundreds of teams. A company's early agile teams carry the burden of destiny. Testing them, just like testing any prototype, should reflect diverse, realistic conditions. The most successful companies focus on vital customer experiences that cause the greatest frustrations among functional silos.

Still, no agile team should launch unless and until it is ready to begin. *Ready* doesn't mean planned in detail and guaranteed to succeed. It means that the team is:

- Focused on a major business opportunity with a lot at stake

- Responsible for specific outcomes

- Trusted to work autonomously—guided by clear decision rights, properly resourced, and staffed with a small group of multidisciplinary experts who are passionate about the opportunity

- Committed to applying agile values, principles, and practices

- Empowered to collaborate closely with customers

- Able to create rapid prototypes and fast feedback loops

- Supported by senior executives who will address impediments and drive adoption of the team's work

Whatever the pace or end point, results should begin showing up quickly. Financial results may take a while—Jeff Bezos believes that most initiatives take five to seven years to pay dividends for Amazon—but positive changes in customer behavior and team problem solving provide early signs that initiatives are on the right track. At the beginning of its agile initiative, the advanced technology group at 3M Health Information Systems launched eight to ten teams every month or two; two years in, more than ninety teams were up and running. 3M's Corporate Research Systems Lab got started later but launched twenty teams in three months. "Agile adoption has already enabled accelerated product deliveries and the release of a beta application six months earlier than originally planned," said Tammy Sparrow, a senior program manager at 3M Health Information Systems.[4]

Harmonizing Bureaucracy and Innovation

The more teams a company launches, the more it is likely to encounter friction between agile and bureaucratic parts of an organization. In the past, people have assumed that the two elements had to be kept separate, because innovation efforts would always be squelched by bureaucracy. That's why so many have dreamed wistfully of ambidextrous leaders, equally adept at running the business and changing the business. It's why so many organizations established skunkworks or separate operating units for disruptive new ventures. Unfortunately, such leaders are scarce, and fledgling skunkworks often die on the vine.

An agile enterprise, however, has to create harmony and complementarity between operations and innovation, and those that are furthest along on the journey have learned how to do so. As we will see in chapter 8, for example, Amazon has built big, innovative businesses in the very heart of its existing organization; it has also structured its bureaucratic functions so that they harmonize with innovation efforts. Agile enterprises typically rely on at least three tools for bringing the two sides into sync.

One of the best ways to overcome the friction—and to set the organization on the right path—is to engage operating people in agile teams. Add some operators as full-time members of teams that need their expertise. Use others as subject matter experts that agile teams can call upon for urgent requests. Launch agile teams with lots of operators to challenge current operating standards and to redesign business processes and technology to create new standards of efficiency and quality. Build trust and collaboration among innovators and operators. Ensure that agile innovations will take hold and scale effectively in real-world operating conditions. Moreover, as operators learn more about agile values and principles, they will likely begin to explore opportunities to apply them to their own functions. The questions on the next page suggest some of the ways a company can help more people understand agile principles and put them to work. The adoption of agile values and principles throughout the organization makes the final step, synchronizing operations and innovations, much easier.

People who work in an organization's support and control functions—the bureaucrats—can also join agile teams and take the values and some of the principles back to their own units, creating what might be called an agile-harmonized bureaucracy. Bureaucratic units may not operate as agile teams, but they can learn to be better bureaucracies. Again, the questions on the next page are good guidelines for bringing about the necessary changes. Bureaucratic leaders can develop more humility. They can show greater willingness to question the value of predictions. They can begin thinking of innovators as their customers. Once learned, agile mindsets often put down roots. When rank-and-file bureaucrats begin posing these questions of their leaders, you will know that agile is likely to flourish.

The agile concept of the sprint is also a powerful device for harmonizing the organization. Sprints offer a quick and inexpensive way to reduce wait times and accelerate adaptation. They turn big, lengthy programs into smaller batches that use rapid feedback loops

TEN QUESTIONS TO ASK AS A COMPANY LAUNCHES MORE AGILE TEAMS

Scaling up agile is always a challenge. The following questions will help you get off on the right foot.

1. Where can we prudently give people greater autonomy and decision authority?

2. Should more employees learn to create backlogs that allow them to prioritize and sequence work?

3. How can people collect more feedback from customers?

4. How can employees minimize work in process?

5. Can we use regular retrospectives to identify better ways of working?

6. Would a fifteen-minute coordination discussion each morning help us help each other?

7. Should we encourage greater collaboration through more team-based metrics and incentives?

8. How can we provide more performance feedback more quickly?

9. Where can we eliminate low-value work?

10. Where can we use experiments and incremental, iterative development?

with customers, internal or external. That allows people working in complex systems to quickly start, stop, or pivot their activities in response to changes or new demands. Sprints act much like clutches in synchronizing large, slow-moving gears with those that are spinning rapidly. When a company uses sprints, breakthrough innovations don't have to be five-year gambles of the sort that terrifies bureaucrats; they become short bursts that can regularly be reviewed and adapted. Similarly, cumbersome planning and funding activities don't have to happen in annual cycles—cycles that force innovation teams to delay their starts or postpone the death of floundering initiatives. Breaking a long, monolithic planning and budgeting process into quarterly sprints minimizes wait times and increases flow efficiency. To increase agility, companies are likely to find opportunities not only in planning and budgeting but also in performance assessments, business process reviews, structural changes, communication programs, and more.

Scaling Agile Frameworks

Before we leave the topic of scaling agile, we should review a few of the frameworks that are available for managing the task. After all, managing agile at scale requires leaders to know enough to define what they mean by agile and what methodology they are going to use. Our clients always want to know: Which methodology is best?

Unfortunately, we have no simple answer. There are dozens of agile frameworks. Certainly, it is easier to manage teams if they all use the same variety of agile, but is it necessary? Can some teams use Scrum while others use Kanban, Extreme Programming (XP), Crystal, Dynamic Systems Development Method (DSDM), or some hybrid method? As always, the answer lies in balance and trade-offs. On the one hand, to force consistency is to impose bureaucracy on agility—a slippery slope. On the other hand, there are real costs to expanding the number of agile frameworks. It raises training expense. It increases the difficulty of transferring people across teams. It interferes with sharing best practices across teams. It raises the costs of coordination and communications, and it increases the complexity of planning multiteam road maps and release dates.

Choosing an approach or two for individual agile teams is relatively easy, and Scrum is likely to be in the mix. (Full disclosure: Scrum Inc. and Scrum@Scale currently have partnerships with Bain & Company.) Scrum has ten times as many users as the runner-up framework, Kanban. Scrum has been tested and refined with tens of thousands of users for more than twenty-five years. It's a flexible framework that combines frequently and easily with other approaches, including Kanban and XP. Scrum training materials are strong, and user tips are plentiful. Nearly all project management software and scaling systems presume their users will be running Scrum teams.

However, choosing a scaling framework is more complicated. Scaling frameworks started popping up only around 2010. Recent user surveys show that the four most popular frameworks are the Scaled Agile Framework (SAFe), "Don't know," Scrum of Scrums (aka Scrum@Scale), and "Internally created methods."[5] In other words, this space is still wide open, and new players continue to emerge. The latest entrants include the Spotify Model, Disciplined Agile Delivery (DAD), Large Scale Scrum (LeSS), Enterprise Scrum, Lean Management, Agile Portfolio Management (APM), Nexus, and Recipes for Agile Governance in the Enterprise (RAGE). You can see why people can get confused.

Describing all of these frameworks or recommending any one of them is beyond the scope of this book. Competitive debates among their supporters often feel more like religious wars than the type of collaborative exchange of ideas that led to the agile manifesto, and those debates will certainly not be resolved in a few paragraphs here. We have worked extensively with most scaling frameworks and can appreciate why they all have ardent fans. But prudent choices are less about which framework is the best and more about which frameworks are best suited to the specific needs of a business. So let's briefly explore some of the strengths, weaknesses, and most favorable operating environments for three of the most popular frameworks.

Scaled Agile Framework (SAFe)

SAFe officially launched in 2011, and has had six major updates as this book goes to press. About 30 percent of companies scaling agile say they use the SAFe framework. It is by far the most detailed and prescriptive approach. First-time visitors to the SAFe website may feel overwhelmed by the volume and specificity of guidance available. (A Google site search shows 2,390 indexed pages on the Scaled Agile Framework website, compared to 41 for Enterprise Scrum.) SAFe builds on a strong Scrum foundation and offers prescriptions for four levels of scaling: teams, programs, large-solutions, and portfolios. Its core premise is that managers should divide innovation work into value streams focused on customer needs. Most value streams deploy five to ten agile teams (50–150 people), known collectively as a release train. If the value stream needs more teams, it adds additional release trains. SAFe introduces several new roles, including lean portfolio managers, epic owners, enterprise architects, solution architects, solution managers, solution train engineers, product managers, system architects, release train engineers, and business owners. It also adds a number of events and artifacts to the scaling of Scrum. Its 2018 release (SAFe 4.6) focused on strengthening five core competencies: lean agile leadership, team and technical agility, the software development practices known as DevOps and release on demand, business solutions and lean systems engineering, and lean portfolio management. (SAFe 5.0 launched in January 2020.)

SAFe's strengths include the depth and breadth of its prescriptions, its training programs, its big-picture view of performance beyond the team level, its appeal to control-oriented executives, and its ability to coordinate interdependencies among teams. It does a nice job developing and managing a complete taxonomy of teams. Many SAFe users rave about the alignment and coordination processes known as program increment (or big room) planning that synchronize teams every eight to twelve weeks. SAFe's weaknesses include the rigidity of its prescriptions, its limited applicability to innovations beyond technology and software development, the amount of time and expense required for planning and coordinating activities, the amount of top-down bureaucracy that carries over to scaling processes, and its lack of attention to the harmonization of support and control functions such as human resources, marketing, and customer services.

Overall, SAFe works most effectively in organizations that have a heavy technology focus combined with monolithic architectures. It works well in companies that fear ambiguity, want to preserve a significant level of top-down control, do not believe they need many breakthrough innovations, and need to synchronize a large number of interdependencies among teams. Of course, SAFe can also work where organizations have enough experience and confidence to customize the process and increase its flexibility to suit their own cultural needs.

Scrum@Scale (Scrum of Scrums)

Jeff Sutherland, the cocreator of Scrum, publicly introduced the Scrum@Scale framework in 2014. However, he is quick to point out that teams of Scrum teams have existed as long as Scrum has—about twenty-five years. Sutherland designed the Scrum@Scale framework to coordinate multiple teams with a "minimum viable bureaucracy" in what he calls a "scale-free architecture." The system is designed to scale across the entire organization—all departments, all products, and all services in all types of organizations. Sutherland intentionally avoids adding complexity that could hurt the productivity of individual Scrum teams. Scrum@Scale simplifies scaling by "using Scrum to scale Scrum"; it expands at a sustainable pace of change as determined by the organization. Compared to SAFe, it aspires to a more comprehensive enterprise transformation with fewer prescriptive processes.

To coordinate interdependencies across teams, the framework regularly brings together the product owners of teams to discuss *what* teams are doing, and it brings the Scrum masters of teams to share *how* they are doing it. In other words, rather than bringing entire teams together for coordination sessions, Scrum@Scale brings representatives from the teams together to manage interdependencies. The framework seeks to build common values of openness, courage, focus, respect, and commitment across the entire organization, using transparency, inspection, and adaptation in the process. An Executive MetaScrum Team serves as the product owner for the entire organization, working with product owners to develop the organizational vision, set the strategic priorities, and align all the teams around common goals. An Executive Action Team serves as the Scrum master for the entire organization, working with Scrum masters to remove constraints that are impeding the progress of teams. The two executive teams use common feedback tools and metrics to connect their work.

Scrum@Scale's strengths include its ambition to improve the agility of the entire organization; the complete consistency of the framework with successful Scrum values, principles, and practices; and reducing the layers and bottlenecks of bureaucracy with very low overhead costs. Its fans also point to its focus on reducing the time required to make decisions and to its high level of transparency, which allows teams to quickly reduce work that fails to create value. Scrum@Scale recognizes the roles of knowledge and infrastructure teams that support Scrum teams but do not formally operate as Scrum teams. The approach's weaknesses include limited specifics and prescribed practices, few techniques for effectively coordinating among large numbers of highly interdependent teams, and limited case examples of enterprise-wide transformation successes. Companies that have been using another framework (such as SAFe) may find it difficult to transition to Scrum@Scale, and will likely decide to keep elements of previous frameworks that they find most helpful.

Overall, Scrum@Scale works most effectively in organizations that are comfortable with Scrum approaches and want to scale them in ways that reinforce fundamental Scrum values and principles. It works well when companies are comfortable with some ambiguity and would like to customize their approach to scaling. It is effective where organizations want more focus on breakthrough innovations than on top-down controls.

The Spotify Model

Spotify, the media-services and audio-streaming provider, could scarcely be clearer about its scaling model. It created the model to scale agile teams in its unique engineering organization and culture. It warns that the model is constantly evolving and should not be copied by other companies, or even by other areas within Spotify. Nevertheless, ever since 2012—the year when Henrik Kniberg and Anders Ivarsson published their paper on scaling agile at Spotify—companies have ignored Spotify's advice, copied its engineering structure, and tried to apply it to their entire enterprise.[6] The result is an upsurge of *squads*, *tribes*, *chapters*, and *guilds*, all Spotify terminology. Squads are like Scrum teams. Tribes are collections of ten or fewer squads (fewer than one hundred people) working on related areas. Chapters are groups of people with similar functional skills who work within the same tribe in matrix fashion. Guilds are informal communities of interest that share knowledge and practices.

The Spotify model is intuitive and easy to understand; it works well in Spotify's engineering department, though it is not a significant factor in areas such as strategic planning or finance. The approach favors strong team autonomy, guided by shared ambitions. It allows teams to develop their own ways of working, encouraging flexibility with agile tools and techniques. As for weaknesses, the model is light on prescriptions. Because Spotify designed its model for a culture that already existed, it did not need to prescribe or change all of the cultural norms and ways of working that make it so effective. Many adopters of the Spotify model assume the key to success is the organization structure. In fact, the organization structure capitalizes on the trust and collaboration inherent in the company's culture. Similarly, the model is light on developing logical taxonomies and managing interdependencies among teams, since Spotify's teams have fewer interdependencies than at most organizations because of its modular products and technology architecture. As a result, companies trying to copy the Spotify model—but that have product lines requiring close coordination of interdependencies—often end up with tribe structures that create chaos. The model does not describe structures, roles, or decision rights for operations, support, and control functions outside of development.

Overall, the Spotify model is effective for innovation departments with cultures and architectures similar to Spotify's. Spotify's engineering culture has always stressed servant leadership, minimization of interdependencies among teams, autonomy, democratic decisions, and innovation over risk avoidance. Adapting the Spotify model to different cultures or different parts of the company requires sophisticated customization.

As these brief overviews demonstrate, models for scaling agile vary significantly. They are likely to succeed in different business and cultural environments. All are helpful for getting to agile at scale, but none has yet shown strong records of accomplishment in creating agile enterprises. Until they do, companies will need to combine, customize, and augment the frameworks to address their unique situations.

FIVE KEY TAKEAWAYS

1. There are major differences in both mindsets and methods between companies that set out to create agile enterprises and those doing agile at scale.

2. Adding dozens or hundreds of agile teams is sufficient to do agile at scale. But if the dominant mindsets and operating systems remain bureaucratic, they will limit agile's potential.

3. Creating an agile enterprise requires balancing and integrating operations with innovation. Agile enterprises run the business reliably and efficiently, change the business to capitalize on unpredictable opportunities, and synchronize the two kinds of activities.

4. The best way to manage the transition to an agile enterprise is to manage it like any other agile team.

5. Companies that create agile enterprises see major changes in their business. Scaling up shifts the mix of work so that the business is doing more innovation relative to routine operations.

3

HOW AGILE DO
YOU WANT TO BE?

Spoiler alert: the title of this chapter is a trick question. You will soon see why. But let's start with a different kind of journey altogether.

In February of 1982, Mark Allen was twenty-four years old and had been out of college for two years. A strong swimmer, he had been working as a lifeguard in San Diego, participating successfully in occasional lifeguard competitions. San Diego was the home of modern-day triathlons, long-distance combinations of swimming, bicycling, and running events. The sport was still new, and many questioned whether it would survive.

But Allen was captivated. That month, he decided he wanted to compete in the sixth Ironman World Championship in Hawaii, coming up in October. It would be a grueling race: a 2.4-mile (3.86 kilometer) swim, followed by a 112-mile (180.25 kilometer) bicycle ride, and then a full 26.22-mile (42.20 kilometer) marathon run.

Allen started by benchmarking how fast the world's best triathletes were running and learned that they were doing close to five-minute miles. So that's what he did. Running at that rate sent his heart rate to 190 beats a minute, but he trusted in the no pain, no gain coaching philosophy of the times. Unfortunately, it didn't work. He entered but did not complete the 1982 event.

For two years thereafter, Allen pushed himself harder and harder. "I went too hard all the time," he later told an interviewer. "Sometimes I did have good results in those races, because you get a certain type of fitness out of that. Long term, it was burning me out, and I was getting some minor injury things that I'd have to take a few days off. After almost every race I ended up getting sick."[1]

Allen then met a coach named Phil Maffetone, who had a different training philosophy. Maffetone recommended working at a challenging but sustainable pace, known as the maximum aerobic heart rate. There are sophisticated methods for determining this level for a particular individual, including expired gas analysis or blood lactate levels, but they require expensive equipment and analysis. Maffetone had developed adequate approximations using a few simple variables such as age, physical conditioning, experience, and medical conditions.

Using these guidelines, Allen determined that his target heart rate should be about 155 beats per minute. Running at 155 beats per minute made him slow down. He went from running 5:30 minute miles to 8:45 minute miles, more than three minutes slower. He felt embarrassed, and he wondered if the training was even working. But he also felt stronger. Instead of dreading his next training session, he began enjoying them:

> I got faster very consistently for about three years and then the very top speed slowed down. At some point you're not going to get any faster. After about three years, at the end of the season I was able to run a 5:30–5:45 pace at 155 beats per minute. . . . What did change is that the fall-off from mile to mile became less over time. You might do your first mile

on the track at 5:30 pace, then the next mile at 5:45, then 6:00, then 6:10, something like that. Over time that fall-off became very small, so I could run two, three, or four miles and the fall-off would only be 10 seconds total, so you start at 5:30, and by the third mile you're still running 5:35–5:40. There are different levels of fitness—there is speed and there is the ability to hold speed over time.[2]

Allen trained his body and mind to deal with the three-hour physiological barrier, then the six-hour barrier. When his performance plateaued, he employed a wide range of techniques to take it to the next level, including speed, strength, and endurance training; nutrition improvements; stress management; and sleep guidelines. All of these became part of his integrated system of continuous improvement.

Seven years after failing to complete his first Ironman competition, Mark Allen won the 1989 Ironman World Championship in an epic battle against Dave Scott. From 1988 to 1990, he won twenty-one consecutive races. By 1995, Allen had won six Ironman competitions. *Triathlete* magazine crowned him "Triathlete of the Year" six times.[3] An ESPN poll voted him the Greatest Endurance Athlete of All Time.

His transition from lifeguard to those lofty heights offers remarkable insights into any human transformation—including the creation of an agile business system. Organizations embarking on a transformation to an agile enterprise are like triathletes in training. It's an ambitious project. There is an optimal pace. It's likely to take years to come to fruition. But successful companies will be able to do things that few others can even contemplate.

As we will see in this chapter, moreover, the challenges are almost directly analogous. So are the pathways that a company must follow if it is to succeed in determining how far—and how fast—it wants to go.

Challenges

Like the optimal heart rate for an athlete, there is an optimal level of change for every business, and for every activity within a business. Ideally, an agile business system would operate at the golden mean between *change deficiency*—leading to a static business system that adapts too slowly to survive—and *change excess*, creating a chaotic business system that constantly risks spinning out of control. When a company is operating in this sweet spot, the benefits of an agile system exceed the costs by the greatest amount, producing the highest net value (the difference between the benefits and the costs of agile) for the business (figure 3-1).

Change Deficiency

Of the two extremes, a static business system is the greater threat for most large companies. Change deficiencies happen more frequently in large organizations, and the impact is more devastating. Bureaucracy slows innovation to a crawl. Sluggish incumbents

FIGURE 3-1

The agile golden mean

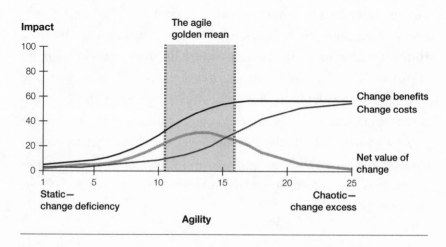

watch innovative insurgents speed past them. Finding the courage and the investment dollars to catch up with the insurgents grows increasingly improbable. That's why the average life span of companies on the S&P 500 list has plummeted from sixty years in the 1950s to less than twenty years today, and experts estimate that it could fall to twelve by 2027.[4] Horror stories of the crippling declines of once-vigorous companies—Eastman Kodak, RadioShack, Polaroid, Blockbuster, Toys "R" Us, and Xerox—drive terrifying fears of death by disruption.

Change Excess

The other extreme, a chaotic business system, is equally dangerous but is more common in small start-ups than in large companies. Research on 3,200 high-growth technology companies shows that the primary cause of failure in fast-moving start-ups is premature scaling—growing too fast before properly validating fundamental business concepts and building repeatable, stabilizing operating systems. Data suggests that start-ups need two or three times as long to validate their market than most founders expect.[5]

Of course, chaotic systems also afflict large-scale companies. Uber, for example, has been extraordinarily innovative, but its early years were plagued by sloppy operating standards, widely reported in the business press at the time.[6] That deficiency led to launching tests of autonomous vehicles without proper permits, false advertising to recruit drivers, accusations of price gouging, claims of sexual harassment, allegations of unethical booking of fake rides at its primary competitor, and privacy violations. Likewise, Tesla's ingenious CEO, Elon Musk, admitted that his impulsive nature, capricious tweets, and lack of operating experience often created chaos for the company. He set production deadlines and price targets for Tesla's Model 3 that seemed impossible to meet, and indeed they were. Problems running the business drove Tesla within days of bankruptcy. Musk told *60 Minutes*, "Well, I mean punctuality's not my strong suit. I think, uh, well, why would people think that if I've been late on all the other models, that I'd be suddenly on time with this one? . . . I never made a mass-produced car. How am I supposed to know with precision when it's going to get done?"[7]

Finding the sweet spot requires estimates of the benefits and costs of increasing agility. Agility can produce extraordinary benefits, but it requires balance, and the trade-offs should be quantified. Even rough estimates of the benefits and costs can help to set realistic expectations for how much is at stake, how far a company's agile transition should go, and how fast it should proceed.

Representative benefits typically include the following:

- *Greater revenue growth* because of better and faster new-product introductions, service improvements, greater pricing power (thanks to higher levels of innovation), new business launches, adding new customers, retaining more customers, and higher customer lifetime values

- *Lower costs* because of more efficient innovation, fewer write-downs of obsolete inventory, greater ability to attract and retain high-quality people, lower employee turnover, higher morale and productivity, and the elimination of unproductive activities

- *Fewer assets* because of less work in process and lower inventory levels

The potential costs vary widely from one company to another, but you may encounter any of the following, and so you will want to estimate their effects:

- *Transition costs*, including the need to invest in new technology, training and coaching costs, and lost productivity while people reorganize and learn new methods and roles

- *Efficiency costs*, such as lower capacity utilization (to speed up response times), decreased economies of scale, duplicated efforts, the cost of less uniformity in some functions, and the cost of greater experimentation

- *Increased risks,* such as the risk of more errors resulting from less oversight of individuals with lower skills and capabilities; and the risk of greater variation around forecasts

- *Organizational costs,* including the cost of coordination across teams, the cost of team colocation, higher turnover of people who don't fit with agile approaches, and the cost of more frequent changes in assignments and matrix reporting structures

Being up-front about these trade-offs helps to set realistic expectations. It also explains why we repeatedly stress the importance of balance and trade-offs while so many agile gurus seem determined to out-crazy each other with increasingly radical and precipitous recommendations.

Here's a tip: Before you embark on an agile journey, go online and search for terms such as "agile doesn't work." You will see more than 40 million results (we are not making up this number). Sample headlines include "Why Isn't Agile Working?," "Back to Waterfall," "Why 'Agile' and Especially Scrum Are Terrible," and "Why People Give Up on Agile." Now, nobody should believe everything (or perhaps anything) that they read on the internet. But you should at least check out some of the criticisms, look for recurring themes, and prepare to deal with the challenges.

Conceptually, navigating within agile's golden mean to avoid the dangers of both deficiencies and excesses seems sensible, even simple. Be aware, however, that the golden mean never lies in exactly the same spot for any two companies. The right balance will vary by industry, company, and activity within a business (see figure 3-2). Furthermore, it is likely to change over time and with experience. This is why two of the most common shortcuts to creating an agile enterprise—copying some other company and big-bang initiatives—rarely work. Launching an all-at-once agile transition, for example,

FIGURE 3-2

Typical conditions (top) and favorable agile conditions (bottom)

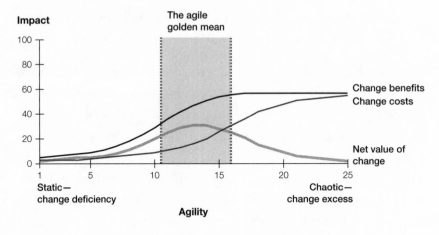

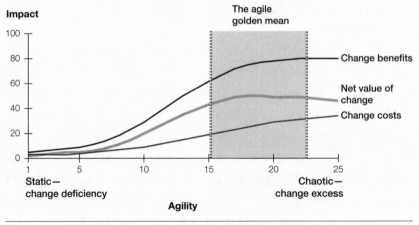

requires a guess at the golden mean. But businesses are complex systems that behave in random, unpredictable ways, and predictions usually fail in vague and uncertain conditions. Anyway, we human beings simply aren't as good at forecasting as we think we are. Dan Lovallo and Daniel Kahneman describe what they call the planning fallacy: people tend to overestimate their own capabilities, exaggerate their ability to shape the future, and underestimate the costs, time, and risks in planning a project.[8] Phil Tetlock, a professor at the University of Pennsylvania's Wharton School and coauthor of *Superforecasting: The Art and Science of Prediction*, suggests that a good starting point is to assume that our predictions are 50 percent accurate, the same as if we were predicting the toss of a coin.[9]

That's why big-bang agile restructurings, trendy as they may be, tend to flounder. Leaders may force nearly everyone into agile squads and tribes. They may place people with agile attitudes but little experience in positions that need expertise. They may try to reduce headcount—especially in support and control functions—by 20 to 30 percent. But the golden mean remains elusive. Researchers have now had more than five years to study the results of such programs. Though companies pursuing this approach often add hundreds or thousands of agile teams and reduce the cost of bureaucracy, their overall business agility and results rarely improve.

Pathways to Success

If copying and guessing don't work, what does? How can a company find its golden mean with the right level of agile and the right rate of change? Think back to Mark Allen. He clarified his goal, winning an Ironman triathlon. He developed critical metrics for tracking his progress. He used those metrics to identify the most important constraints, and he constantly adjusted his program to push through barriers and plateaus. He was thus able to create an integrated system that helped him develop at the proper pace. Let's look at each of these elements in the context of a business organization.

Determining Your Purpose

Allen didn't want to get in shape to win more lifeguard competitions, or to lose weight, or to win bodybuilding contests. He wanted to win the Ironman World Championship. Companies need to be equally clear. No company should want to be agile for the sake of being more agile. Agile is a means to an end, and the end is likely to be different for every organization. The tighter the organizational alignment around a clear and shared purpose, the easier it is to trust autonomous teams to do the right things without micromanagement. That's because everyone is committed to the purpose behind the plans and can adapt effectively to unexpected circumstances.

How you express your company's purpose matters a great deal. Warby Parker puts it like this: "To offer designer eyewear at a revolutionary price, while leading the way for socially conscious businesses."[10] The people at Warby Parker enjoy significant freedom because the goal is so easy to understand. Barnes & Noble, on the other hand, expressed its purpose this way for many years:

> Our mission is to operate the best specialty retail business in America, regardless of the product we sell. Because the product we sell is books, our aspirations must be consistent with the promise and the ideals of the volumes which line our shelves. To say that our mission exists independent of the product we sell is to demean the importance and the distinction of being booksellers.
>
> As booksellers we are determined to be the very best in our business, regardless of the size, pedigree or inclinations of our competitors. We will continue to bring our industry nuances of style and approaches to bookselling which are consistent with our evolving aspirations.
>
> Above all, we expect to be a credit to the communities we serve, a valuable resource to our customers, and a place where our dedicated booksellers can grow and prosper. Toward this end we will not only listen to our customers and booksellers but embrace the idea that the Company is at their service.[11]

No matter how many times you read the statement, it doesn't get any easier to understand. Can you imagine agile teams at the company being left on their own to implement that purpose?

There are a couple of purposes, incidentally, that are bad ideas from the beginning: Wanting to be part of a trendy management philosophy. Chopping headcounts without innovating business processes and then blaming the resulting layoffs on agile. It's better not to do agile at all than to do it for the wrong reasons.

Learning to Measure Agility

Plenty of executives these days would like their companies to be more agile. Some have set up pilots to give it a try. But in our experience, few know how to accurately assess their current positions or track their progress. Nor do they know what to change, or by how much, to improve the organization's agility. Some have decided to count the number of agile teams that are up and running. Others report the number of people that have been trained in agile techniques. Only a handful measure the impact of agility on cash flows and shareholder value. (Of course, some agile fanatics condemn even measuring shareholder value, which is ridiculous. Just because shareholder value isn't all that matters doesn't mean it shouldn't matter at all.)

The problem here is easily stated: there are no simple metrics that every company can use to assess its current agility or its progress toward greater agility. Instead, companies must develop their own customized indicators, testing—in good agile fashion—the relationships among the system's major components, including inputs, activities, outputs, outcomes, and purposes (figure 3-3). So let's begin by understanding those components:

- *Purposes* are the ultimate missions and ambitions of an agile enterprise. They are the long-term cumulative effects of an agile business system, such as Warby Parker's ambition to lead the way for socially conscious businesses.

- *Outcomes* are the shorter-term changes and benefits that are achieved by agile activities and outputs, typically in one to

FIGURE 3-3

Five kinds of metrics

Inputs	Activities	Outputs	Outcomes	Purposes
Resources available to create results	*Actions and processes used to generate results*	*What activities produce; the direct, immediate results of activities performed*	*Changes and benefits; achieved by the activities and outputs*	*Long-term, cumulative effects of activities, outputs, and outcomes*
• Appropriate numbers and allocations of qualified agile experts	• Senior leaders act as an agile team, trust and empower people, and obsess over customers	• Higher quality products and services	• Improved market share and revenue growth	• Measurable progress toward achieving the company's mission and ambitions
• Adequate agile training and coaching skills	• Teams embrace agile values and scale effectively	• Decision speed and faster time to market	• Improved shareholder value	
• Organization structures, cultures, and technology architectures that facilitate agile practices	• Operations partner well with agile teams	• Increased team productivity and morale	• Improved profitability	
• Conducive facilities	• Management systems support agile values and practices	• More sustainable workloads	• Improved customer advocacy and behaviors	
			• Improved employee engagement	

Source: Adapted from the *W. K. Kellogg Foundation Logic Model Development Guide,* https://www.wkkf.org/resource-directory/resource/2006/02/wk-kellogg-foundation-logic-model-development-guide (accessed January 22, 2020).

three years. They include results such as changes in market share, revenue, shareholder value, profitability, customer buying behaviors, and team productivity.

- *Outputs* are the direct, immediate results of work. Common examples of agile outputs include higher quality products and services, shorter decisions, faster development cycles and time to market, and increased team productivity and morale. Are parts of the company not operating in agile teams nonetheless embracing agile values and accelerating change? Is the operating model enhancing agility rather than undermining it? Is the entire system collaborating more effectively? You can't take outputs to the bank, but you can use them to determine whether activities are producing results that should lead to positive outcomes.

- *Activities* are the actions and processes that generate outputs. They include the actions of senior executives, agile teams, operations, and support and control functions. Are senior leaders using agile practices in their own work? Are they trusting and empowering people? Are they creating a culture that focuses obsessively on customers and adapts quickly to customers' changing needs? Are the most talented and innovative people working on agile teams? Do the teams adhere consistently to agile values, principles, and practices? Are agile teams deployed in every area where they should be deployed? Are planning, budgeting, and resource allocation processes frequent and flexible enough to quickly shift resources to the company's highest priorities?

- *Inputs* are the resources available to help create results. They include financial resources, the quantity and quality of agile experts, organizational structures, software tools, and technology architectures. What is the company's level of experience with agile methods? What are the leaders' mindsets and cultural norms? What are the company's technology capabilities? Industry conditions are another key input: businesses that are particularly turbulent, such as technology, medical products, and retail, require more adaptive innovation than industries such as basic materials or the public sector. Strategic priorities are important as well. For instance, strategies that focus on cost leadership and scale require less agility than strategies focusing on innovation.

Together, these components create the agile business system. Doing agile right means skillfully combining them to perpetually pursue the company's purposes, even in volatile and unpredictable conditions. *Measuring* agile requires developing metrics in each area.

We realize that all this may sound a little complicated. In reality, it's just a way of organizing, visualizing, and helping you address existing complexities in ways that make them more manageable. To improve results, you need to understand where results come from and then improve the processes that cause them. The trick is learning to analyze dynamic systems in just enough detail to be insightful, without being overwhelming—finding balance, in short, and relying once again on the minimum viable solution.

An example may help. One of our retail clients was excited about the growing number of agile teams in its organization and a corresponding increase in revenue growth. But when the people there analyzed what was going on in terms of the various elements, they found some surprises. Revenues (an important outcome) were growing because industry growth was accelerating. But the company's share of that growth (a more important outcome) was declining. Its existing core customers were as loyal as ever, but it was failing to attract the large and rapidly growing segment of next-generation shoppers. Those shoppers were not impressed by traditional forms of marketing or merchandising. They wanted faster and more reliable online deliveries. They wanted an in-store shopping experience that focused less on brands and more on solutions, such as more natural forms of skin care (outputs). There was an agile supply-chain team, but it concentrated on boosting the efficiency of traditional warehouses rather than improving both cost and speed by offering better options for shoppers to buy online and immediately pick up orders in stores (activities). There were no agile teams focused on buying the right brands, on developing the right displays, or on providing the best service experiences (more activities) for those shoppers. Worse yet, the teams had no members who represented, or even understood, the needs of the next generation (inputs). Once these cause-and-effect relationships were understood, agile teams pounced on them, improving inputs, activities, outputs, outcomes, and purposes.

Use Agile Methods to Determine How Agile to Be

By now, it should be clear why the chapter heading—"How Agile Do You Want to Be?"—was a trick question. At the beginning of an agile journey, it is nearly impossible to predict the answer. Predicting, commanding, and controlling is a hazardous approach to any innovation but especially to the design and development of a new business system. Ironically, senior executives who expect hundreds or thousands of agile teams to follow agile principles and practices sometimes revert instinctively to bureaucratic methods to envision, develop, and implement the new system. There's an old saying, dubiously attributed to Albert Einstein, that we cannot solve problems with the same level of thinking that created them. Nevertheless, that is exactly how too many executives approach agile transformations. The missteps take many forms:

- Instead of demonstrating intellectual humility and admitting that the guiding vision is a working prototype that will adapt with experience, leaders attempt to maximize the motivation for change by pretending to have all the answers. They impose inflexible organizational structures. They burn the boats to quell any questions about commitment.

- Instead of recognizing front-line employees as leadership's most important customers—the people who should collaborate on the innovation process and must ultimately make the system work—executives plot in secret war rooms and unveil the changes through public press releases.

- Instead of viewing feedback from the most experienced employees as valuable opportunities for improvement, leaders regard their opinions as criticisms from recalcitrant resisters who must be fixed or fired.

- Instead of responding to change, program management offices build complex Gantt charts with bright red dots to flag people who deviate from plans.

The value of the metrics above is their ability to focus corrective actions on true constraints. There is always at least one constraint to further progress, but there are usually fewer constraints than most people imagine. Focusing on fixing problems that are not constraints will not improve throughput and is often a waste of time, money, and energy. This is why the rush to reorganize is always less useful than leaders expect. It is usually a cover for other problems, and it typically creates more trauma than value.

Most often, restructuring is only a euphemism for major layoffs. Have you ever wondered how and why companies bounce from decentralization to centralization and back again, each time announcing layoffs to reduce costs? Or why they pursue other sorts of organizational back-and-forthing, such as changing from functional organizations to product organizations to matrix organizations, and around again? How can every change drive more cost reduction? The reason, typically, is that the executive team sets a cost quota first and only then designs an organization structure to hit it, leaving operators to deal with the consequences. Agile transitions may eventually lead to organizational changes, even continuous ones. But organization structures are almost never the primary constraint, and companies seldom require (or benefit from) immediate wholesale layoffs.

Agile itself offers so many ways to advance an agile transition with greater value and lower cost. Focus the fixes on the real bottlenecks. Get the leadership team to behave like an agile team. Clarify a common ambition. Not enough? Stop activities that customers don't want and teams can't deliver. Replace ineffective innovation groups with agile teams. Still not enough? Shift planning and budgeting to simpler processes at shorter intervals. Focus support and control functions on changing their business processes to better satisfy their internal customers. If the system is still unbalanced, provide more frequent feedback on performance. If these simpler solutions work, you may be able to pursue continuous improvements while postponing or avoiding some of the most expensive and painful solutions.

Change levers such as these essentially become the backlog of the agile leadership team. The leadership team is developing a new, highly innovative agile system, and these are the features that will ultimately come together to make the system work. Like any other agile team, the leadership team prioritizes, sequences, and harmonizes these activities to create the greatest value at the lowest cost. Members work together as a multidisciplinary group to create the system, break through impediments, and pivot as unexpected results develop. We think of the process as much like that of a skilled music mixing engineer, part artist and part scientist. If the treble is too harsh but is very hard to change, you tame it by turning up the base. You don't change more than you need to, since that creates other problems that will then require fixes that will require additional fixes (figure 3-4; see appendix B for definitions).

All of these levers can be valuable when applied to the right problems, in the right sequence, in the right ways. We cannot detail all

FIGURE 3-4

Balancing the agile enterprise operating model

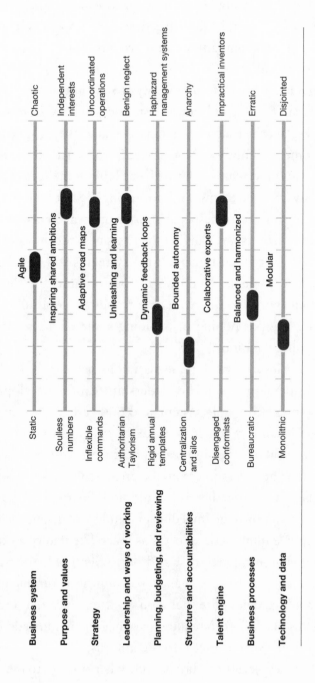

of the possibilities in this book, but we will discuss how to use several of the most popular change management techniques in chapters 4 through 8.

Nearly twenty years before the agile manifesto appeared, a young Mark Allen was discovering the manifesto's principles and practices for himself. His purpose was to win the Ironman World Championship. But achieving that purpose required him to hit a moving target. The first winner of the Ironman, in 1978, completed the course in 11:46:58. By February of 1982, when Allen tried to train by copying the results of leading competitors, the winner finished in 9:19:41, and the man in second place finished in 9:36:57. Benchmarking was not only producing extreme physical and mental exhaustion, it was also limiting Allen's potential. When he won his first Ironman Championship in 1989, he finished in 8:09:14 to achieve his goal.[12] That's more than three and a half hours faster than the pioneers. Allen learned to train by setting a challenging but sustainable pace. He was patient, and he took a long-term perspective. As he exercised at his optimal pace, his performance steadily improved.[13]

Senior executives could choose worse analogies than imagining themselves and their organizations as triathletes in training. The maximum aerobic heart rate is the organization's sustainable pace of change. Instead of tools and techniques such as strength training or nutrition improvements to break through performance plateaus, there are leadership behaviors, cultural norms, planning and funding systems, organization structures, people development, business processes, and technology. We'll discuss how to prioritize, sequence, and implement these techniques in the following chapters.

FIVE KEY TAKEAWAYS

1. More agile is not always better agile. There is an optimal range of agility for every business and for every activity within a business.

2. It is nearly impossible to predict the right range at the beginning of an agile transition. At that point, what you are trying to develop and how you should develop it are not just unknown, they are unknowable. Too many variables are changing too rapidly and too randomly. Rarely will bureaucratic approaches succeed in such conditions. You must develop and implement the agile business system as a perpetual agile innovation program—testing, learning, and continually adapting as you would on any other agile team.

3. Effective agile programs adapt to empirical feedback about inputs, activities, outputs, outcomes, and purposes. Few organizations currently have sufficient data to assess their present level of agility or their progress in improving it.

4. Identifying and quantifying the potential benefits and costs of creating an agile business system is difficult but well worth the effort. Chances are high that the estimates will be inaccurate. That's OK. They will be sufficient to answer many different questions, such as how much value is at stake and how much investment of time and financial resources is worthwhile.

5. Use agile methods to manage agile transitions. Imagine yourself and your organization as triathletes in training. Set a challenging but sustainable pace. Be patient, and take a long-term perspective. As you reach performance plateaus, learn to deploy a wide range of tools and techniques to break through impediments and shift performance to the next level.

4

AGILE LEADERSHIP

Bosch Power Tools is a major division of the big German technology company, with about 20,000 employees in over sixty countries and €4.6 billion in 2018 revenue. Henk Becker, who became CEO in 2019, launched its agile transformation in 2016. He established a six-person team reporting to him that would guide and support the division's six business units, sales organizations, and headquarters during the process.

Three years later, a visitor could see signs of thoroughgoing transformation in the division's everyday operations. The business unit for professional power tools in industrial markets, for instance, established a three-level Kanban process. Stand-up meetings at the product level fed stand-up meetings at the business owner level, which then fed a stand-up meeting at the business unit level. Daniela Kraemer, business owner for power tools solutions in light drilling and chiseling, described her meeting this way: "We share all the project updates in a short period of time. We have tickets on a Kanban board. If you have an update, you turn the item on the board. Then we quickly move on, or we schedule a separate meeting if it's a bigger topic we need to discuss." The meeting includes between eight and ten individuals—product owners and expertise owners, such as supply chain and marketing. It takes thirty minutes, and it starts and ends punctually. "At first people thought, whoa, this is a lot of time," said Kraemer. "But it saves a lot of time."[1]

At the business unit level, leaders constituted themselves an agile leadership team and canceled most existing meetings. Zero-basing the calendar in this way forced them to commit to a new way of working. Business-unit stand-ups took place every Tuesday and Thursday at 4:00 p.m. A giant seven-meter board tracked every major work effort. A team that needed something would turn the item on the board ninety degrees. Leaders could also mark an item for discussion. A Scrum master facilitated the meetings. There was no fixed agenda. Meetings ran between fifteen and thirty minutes, with no item taking more than three minutes. (If there was a need for more discussion among some participants, the thirty minutes following the meeting were kept free.) Team members captured every new idea on the board as a backlog, and every three months held a special meeting to prioritize topics. Everyone could see the ideas of others—incremental EBIT, start of launch, whatever they might be. The transparency and resulting alignment carried over from one meeting to the next, speeding up decisions.

The last of Bosch Power Tools' six business units went through its agile transformation in 2018. By 2019, Becker had established an agile leadership team at the executive level and installed an agile master to support the team. This group defined fourteen focus topics to implement the division's strategy and deployed these throughout the organization as key performance indicators. Becker held his own stand-up meeting every Monday. Members discussed broad organizational topics, ensuring alignment on priorities and individual responsibilities. "In the past we would come with certain topics, but it was not always clear how they were aligned with the strategy," Becker told us. "We always disturbed the teams' sprints. Now we have a clearly defined method of aligning sprints, so that no one is disturbing anyone else."[2]

Becker also changed the strategy process to be more inclusive; giving entrepreneurial responsibility to teams meant that more people were needed to discuss strategy and business issues. Power Tools typically holds two big management meetings a year. Before, these included twenty leaders; now they include 120. In the spring 2019 meeting, Becker spent the first day on leadership, building soft skills, and the second day on strategy topics. By all accounts, he got rave reviews from the division's fifty-five business owners, who were now insiders for the first time.

Business leadership has never been easy, and it doesn't matter whether you're the CEO or a manager lower down in the chain of command.

In the old days, a century or more ago, leaders at least knew what they were supposed to do. Find people to do the required jobs. Tell them what to do. Make sure they did exactly as they were told. Frederick W. Taylor's scientific management codified this approach. Industrial engineers would map out efficient work processes, and bosses would ensure that the work was done. Over time, of course, much of that changed. Many jobs became more complex. Many workers brought skills and opinions of their own and didn't take as readily to instruction. Douglas McGregor's famous Theory Y—which he distinguished from the old, tell-'em-what-to-do Theory X—encapsulated a different kind of management style, one that was said to be more appropriate to the new environment. Listen, don't tell. Trust and believe in your people. Encourage them to take responsibility.[3]

But though business schools and corporate cultures often gave lip service to the tenets of Theory Y, executives and managers often fell back on a kinder, gentler Theory X. They might not yell or order people around, but there was no doubt who was making the decisions. And why shouldn't they? After all, they would be graded and rewarded on hard-to-fudge metrics. They had to hit their sales goals, their cost objectives, their budgets. They had to predict what was coming down the pike and respond appropriately. CEOs—and by extension, boards of directors and shareholders—didn't want to hear excuses; they wanted to see results. So leaders plunged into the work, rolled up their sleeves, told their underlings exactly what to do, and, if need be, did it themselves. Like the factory overseers of old, they knew that their job was to make sure the work got done.

As everyone keeps reminding us, however, times have changed still more. In recent years, it has become harder for leaders to maintain this style of management. Predictability? Forget it. The world is changing too fast. New competitors are cropping up all over. Technology continues to evolve, often too quickly for comfort. Up-and-coming managers and young functional specialists seem to expect more than a company—any company—can give them. Opportunities for growth. More money. Work-life balance. Leaders who were successful at running things in the 1990s or 2000s—which is why they were promoted to ever-more-responsible leadership roles—can now find themselves adrift. Little wonder that so many feel that they are working harder and having less to show for it. Little wonder, too, that they get a nagging suspicion, now and then, that they might be going about things all wrong.

Henk Becker of Bosch Power Tools got that suspicion early on. He had joined Bosch right out of school, with a degree in mechanical engineering. Starting in the company's automotive division, he worked his way up over the years by building his technical skills and competencies. Back then, success meant being the best functional leader he could be, guiding people in what to do. He spent more than twenty years in such roles, and in 2013 joined the executive board of Power Tools. Initially focused on engineering and quality, he added manufacturing and ultimately became CEO of the division in 2019.

By his own account, however, something at Power Tools was different. A few courageous leaders began to give him feedback of a sort he had never heard before. His leadership style, they said, wasn't helping him succeed. It wasn't helping to bring out the best in people, and it wasn't helping Power Tools win in the marketplace. They told him how they wanted to be led differently, complete with examples. The experience, he says now, was "a click in my brain and in my heart." He decided that he needed to change his attitude and his behavior. So he began a process of self-reflection and awareness building. He asked for more feedback. At first his teams were dubious: Was this just a passing fad, or was it real? Slowly, he was able to build trust, and he was able to broaden the group of people actively giving him feedback.

Becker shifted his focus to concentrate on the potential and strength of his people and the organization. He tried not to focus on deficits, he says. He started using positive language. He began asking, "How can we?" instead of probing to understand why something couldn't be done. He focused on listening and two-way communication instead of providing one-way direction. To reinforce his commitment, he gave up his office and parking spot. He also stopped asking people to bring him PowerPoint presentations; instead, he began going out to teams and relying on the information that they were already using. It took time, he says, but he became a different leader—the kind who could successfully launch an agile transformation.

The Starting Point: Reshaping the "Noble Mission," or How Leaders Add Value

Nearly all the executives and managers we encounter are dedicated, hardworking individuals, just as Becker was during his earlier career at Bosch. They take their jobs seriously, and they are committed to helping their company succeed. They might not put it in these terms, but many see themselves on a kind of noble mission. They believe that they create a great deal of value by knowing exactly what needs to be done and getting people to do it. Their role, as they understand it, is to protect their employees from doing things wrong, from wasting time, from screwing up. Their goal is to get the work done as best as it can be done, as quickly as possible, and at the lowest possible cost. Without their hands-on guidance, they think, people would be forever spinning their wheels.

When we help a company launch an agile transformation, we encourage leaders to think carefully about four principles, and about what they mean for leadership behaviors. Doing so begins to shift what leaders believe about that noble mission and about how they add value. As Becker's example shows, changing how you lead requires both effort and discipline. The following principles are good starting points.

Employees Learn by Doing Things Themselves

We have all read, in recent years, about the phenomenon of helicopter parenting, also known as lawnmower or snowplow parenting. Helicopter parents love their children. They recall their own struggles as kids, and they want their own children to be more successful and happier than they themselves were. So they swoop in, as on a helicopter, whenever a difficulty arises. They meet with teachers and principals and coaches, hoping to remove obstacles and smooth the way for their children's success. They hold the difficult conversations and try to resolve things, rather than expecting the children to cope. On one level, the parents' thinking is incontrovertible: they are almost always better than their kids would be at talking to the coach or writing the college essay. On another level, it's easy to see the costs involved. Children don't learn that they can take care of themselves. They don't build the necessary skills. At worst, they run to mommy or daddy for help at every little bump in the road.

Employees are not children, but leaders often treat them the way helicopter parents treat their kids. Leaders don't trust their employees to do the job right, so they give those employees specific, detailed directives. If they have to, they do the job themselves. Some of the employees, like some children of helicopter parents, adopt a kind of learned passivity and wait for the boss to tell them what to do. Those with more talent or spunk—the ones who can see for themselves what to do or how to do it, often better than with traditional objectives and methods—typically bridle at being given detailed instructions. Some are likely to leave. Tufts University professor Amar Bhidé studied the Inc. 500, a compilation of the fastest growing privately held companies in the United States.[4] Many successful company founders explained to him that they had tried to launch a particular venture while at their old job but had been prevented from doing so.

In an agile environment, leaders take a different approach. They may tell a team what to focus on, but never how to do it. Figuring out the *how* is up to team members themselves. Their job is to experiment, to test and learn. What product is most likely to succeed in the marketplace? How can the order-entry process be revamped to ensure both speed and accuracy? What is the best way to ensure a continual stream of qualified candidates for our various departments? Questions like these rarely have easy answers. Leaders may have strong, experience-based opinions about what the answers are, but they usually have no way of knowing whether they are right. Like children, adults learn best by trying things out and seeing what works. That is the hallmark of an agile team.

Trust Is Built over Time

Trust between leaders and the people they lead was an essential part of McGregor's Theory Y. Trust, he said, means the following: "'I know that you will not—deliberately or accidentally, consciously or unconsciously—take unfair advantage of me.' It means 'I can put my situation at the moment, my status and self-esteem in the group, our relationship, my job, my career, even my life in your hands with complete confidence.'"[5] This is a tall order, and McGregor's strictures about trust have most often been observed in the breach. It's tough for a leader to trust a subordinate when the leader isn't sure about the subordinate's intentions or skills. And it's tough for a subordinate to trust a leader who seems to prioritize (at all costs) getting the job done exactly according to his or her directives.

Agile provides a way of building trust—of making people trustworthy, so to speak—over time. Think again about how the method works. An agile team is resourced and given a mission by a leader. Team members break the work up into manageable components, create a backlog, and then begin working their way through the backlog in (say) two-week sprints, reprioritizing over time as may be necessary. At the end of every two weeks both the leader and the team can see what has been accomplished and can learn from it. The process is wholly transparent. Even a cynic would have to agree: How much trouble can a team get itself into in just two weeks—especially if they are taking guidance from the customers they serve? A leader who feels that team members have veered off track can quickly steer them back in a more productive direction by asking: What are our key assumptions and how can we test them? Leading with trust in this manner takes discipline, especially under stress, as that is when control instincts kick in. But it gets easier with time.

Workplace trust, in short, isn't something that exists or doesn't exist in the abstract. It's something that people build by collaborating productively. People on an agile team take on new tasks and assume responsibility for the results. That's how they become trustworthy.

Doing What Only You Can Do Makes Everyone Better Off

In 1817, the English economist David Ricardo published a book called *On the Principles of Political Economy and Taxation*.[6] It elucidated a theory that has since been taught to every first-year economics student and that explains the benefits of international trade.

In principle, said Ricardo, a country could decide to make everything for itself, within its own borders, and not trade with anyone. But its citizens will be better off if they focus on producing whatever they are best at and then trade with countries that produce what *they* are best at. Each has a comparative advantage relative to the other.

Now put this in a managerial context. It's sometimes the case that a manager, by virtue of skills and experience, can do almost everything better than his or her direct reports. At Bosch, Becker may have been the best engineer, the best product designer, the best assessor of exactly what kinds of features would most appeal to customers. But if he were to spend all his time doing those tasks, there's a big opportunity cost: he would not be spending time on the tasks that only he could do. He wouldn't be thinking about the overall direction of the business. He wouldn't be exploring new markets or looking into potential acquisitions. Rather, he would be doing what his employees should be doing, and everyone would be the worse off.

Customers Are the Best Judges of What They Want

Certainly there are plenty of business leaders, from CEOs on down, who believe they have a firm grip on customer needs. The best ones, of course, spend time talking with their customers, so they have at least some evidence on which to base their judgments. Still, it's difficult for any one person, no matter how experienced or intuitive, to know how a customer will respond to any particular feature. It's also difficult for senior leaders to know how internal customers—the people who rely on the work of the IT department, HR, finance, the warehouse, and so on—might want things done differently and how they might respond to innovations.

An agile team assumes that the best judge of what the customer wants is the customer. It's why teams develop minimum viable products—just so they can get customer reactions and can modify the product accordingly. Agile teams working on internal process innovations typically engage the people who will use those innovations as part of the team, so that customer feedback is built in from the very beginning. The representative on the team can consult with his or her peers in the relevant unit and bring the team ongoing feedback about what's looking good and what's falling flat.

The Goal: A Different Kind of Noble Mission (and a Different Way of Adding Value as a Leadership Team)

Agile leaders who think carefully about the issues we just raised—and who adjust their actions accordingly, as Becker did—are apt to find themselves in a very different place from where they started out. They will no doubt be just as dedicated and hardworking as they were originally. But their roles will have changed dramatically, and they will have a very different conception of how they add value to the organization. When leaders on a management team come together in this new way, they can redefine their noble mission still further.

For one thing, they can stop running their business. Think about this for a moment. Most senior leaders spend their time solving problems, watching their budgets, and so on. But what if they now have a dozen or a score or even a hundred agile teams peppered throughout the organization, each one charged with pursuing innovations that will create new opportunities, improve efficiency, and eliminate problems? These leaders no longer need to spend their time doing what they were doing before, because other people are taking on those responsibilities. Instead, they can pursue their own comparative advantage, which is to think about the big picture and make decisions about strategy and resource allocations.

Of course, they can't do that alone. That's why companies that are launching an agile transformation typically reconstitute the executive committee at the top of the organization into an agile leadership team. They do the same with teams of leaders at lower levels of the organization. They thus redefine not only how leaders spend their time but also how they work together.

Today, most companies' executive committees are representative bodies. Business-unit heads and functional heads come together as representatives of their own silos, reporting on their units' accomplishments and looking out for those interests. They may make decisions that benefit their own budgets, that protect talent they are hoarding, or that further their own career aspirations. The CEO or general manager is responsible for weighing each silo's interests and making trade-offs, creating a unified strategy for the good of the whole.

But what happens when the executive committee constitutes itself as an agile leadership team? Doing so means operating as an agile team in service of external and internal customers. Since operating skills and innovating skills seldom thrive together in a single person, the agile leadership team capitalizes on the power of a group. It is a team of decision makers who focus on the greater good, not a collection of individuals. Operational reviews still happen, but they focus on learning, prioritizing, and removing roadblocks. Sometimes operating experts take the lead, and sometimes innovation specialists take the lead. But both groups must collaborate to run the business efficiently and reliably, change the business adaptively, and harmonize all these activities. The agile leadership team brings running the business and changing the business together in proper balance.

Members of a good agile leadership team realize that they create the greatest value for their enterprise not by increasing the number of times they predict, command, and control but by unleashing the untapped potential of tens of thousands of employees. They get comfortable delegating testable decisions and helping to make more decisions testable by those closest to the front line. They help the entire organization build testing and learning skills. They think in terms of systems—creating small, minimum viable microcosms of full systems. These microcosms enable leaders to test multiple changes to see how they interact with one another over time without putting the enterprise at risk. While bureaucrats fear that testing potential changes to the company's operating model will tip their hand and scare people, agile practitioners test almost everything all the time and expect that the organization will grow accustomed to continuous adaptation. They focus on accelerating cycle times and minimizing waiting times, especially the time required for making decisions. They avoid running decisions through excruciating gauntlets up and down the hierarchy. They break complex processes such as planning, budgeting, and new product deployment into smaller, more frequent batches and feedback loops.

The agile leadership team deeply respects the realities of navigating complex systems. It recognizes the futility of long-term forecasting, knowing that transitioning to an agile enterprise is more like driving on a treacherous mountain road in the dark of a rainy night than barreling down a desert straightaway in broad daylight. Team members know where they hope to arrive, but they avoid committing to specific turns beyond the insights of their headlights. They jointly and adaptively determine how far to go, how fast to go, and how to handle unexpected rocks in the road.

The agile leadership team, in short, becomes a strategy team guiding the entire organization, with all of its members looking out for the company's best interests rather than the interests of their individual silos. Members' time horizons shift. They focus on longer-term objectives having to do with building the organization's capabilities rather than worrying about short-term results. Instead of improving the productivity of only their direct reports, they are improving the productivity of thousands of people throughout the entire organization. How do you shift mindsets from being a silo leader to being a member of an agile leadership team? For day-to-day guidance, we often suggest that leadership teams customize and commit to their own version of an agile manifesto. You can see a representative example of a manifesto in appendix A.

Leading the Agile Transformation

As the long list of commitments in appendix A suggests, leading an agile transition is a lot of work. The journey typically begins with the team developing a guiding vision and using it to communicate the potential benefits of an agile enterprise. The team doesn't develop the vision behind closed doors, then spring it on the organization as commandments written in stone. Rather, it views those who will implement agile activities as customers. Like all agile teams, leaders collaborate with their customers and cocreate the vision and potential strategies for achieving it with them in full transparency. They then discuss alternative directions the vision could take, and they identify the key questions that must be answered to determine which of those directions will be most successful. Ideally, they demonstrate intellectual humility. They jointly develop metrics for inputs, activities, outputs, outcomes, and purposes that will help them to monitor and adapt to the answers to those questions.

The transition is a perpetual improvement process, not a project with a completion date. The agile transition is not a costly distraction; it is the way the business will run. The best way to lead an agile transformation is from a mindset of trust rather than one of control. Contrary to conventional wisdom and Hollywood action movies, dictatorial management is ineffective in a crisis. Command-and-control systems work best when operations are stable and predictable, commanders have greater knowledge of operating conditions and potential solutions than their subordinates do, centralized decision makers can effectively handle peak decision volumes, and sticking to standard operating procedures is more important than adapting to change. None of these conditions exists in extreme events such as natural disasters, terrorist attacks, major military battles, or large-scale business transitions. The variability and unpredictability of events are too high for rigid directives. Experienced operators in the field have better knowledge and more current information than remote dictators or their mercenary agents do. Information overloads paralyze command centers, creating devastating bottlenecks. Standard operating procedures fail because the situations are by definition nonstandard.

Managers who fall prey to the dictator-in-a-crisis myth pay a heavy price. Their responses to unexpected developments are slow and ill-informed (think of Hurricane Katrina, the Chernobyl meltdown, perhaps even the ongoing disaster at Sears). And their obvious lack of confidence in front-line employees will hinder growth long after the crisis passes. For these reasons, even modern crisis teams are turning from command-and-control systems to more adaptive, agile approaches.

In a conventional urgent transformation, a small team of people at the top tries to figure out a company's problems and make the necessary changes. In an agile transition, hundreds or even thousands of employees attack those problems at the root—and learn skills they can put to work for the rest of their careers.

During the transition, agile leadership teams help people to make decisions faster and with less information than traditional teams. To do so, they typically take five actions:

1. *They communicate—even overcommunicate—the strategic ambition to a broader range of people.* Since leaders know they will be delegating far more decisions than in the past, they ensure that people making those decisions are fully aligned on what to do and *why* to do it. That way, how they do it can be flexible yet faithful to the strategy.

2. *They build decision makers.* In a turnaround, people are afraid to make mistakes, so they bring decisions to their bosses. Strong leaders act as coaches and trainers to expand the quantity and quality of decision makers.

3. *They strengthen lines of communication among the teams.* To avoid becoming a bottleneck, they develop tools that help everyone see what all the teams are doing at any time.

4. *They accelerate learning loops, emphasizing progress over perfection.* They embrace unpredictability and don't get slowed by excessive precision. Adequate approximations will do.

5. *They shift measurement and reward systems to larger teams.* One of the biggest problems in a crisis is that people focus on doing what is best for the individuals they know and trust, which often means people in their own silos. Effective turnaround leaders enlarge circles of trust and collaboration.

Of course, the agile leadership team has responsibility for determining how far and how fast to go with agile. In keeping with agile principles, it doesn't plan every detail in advance. Even though they have laid out a vision, leaders recognize that they do not yet know how many teams they will require, how quickly they should add them, and how they can best address bureaucratic constraints without throwing the organization into chaos. So they typically launch an initial wave of agile teams, gather data on the value those teams create and the constraints they face, and then decide whether, when, and how to take the next step. This lets them weigh the value of increasing agility (in terms of financial results, customer outcomes, and employee performance) against its costs (in terms of both financial investments and organizational challenges). If the benefits outweigh the costs, leaders build on the momentum and continue to scale up agile—deploying another wave of teams, unblocking constraints in less agile parts of the organization, and repeating the cycle. If not, they can explore ways to increase the value of the agile teams already in place (for instance, removing organizational barriers or upgrading prototyping capabilities) and decrease the costs of change (by publicizing agile successes or hiring experienced agile enthusiasts).

A good agile leadership team avoids bureaucratic arguments to treat an urgent agile transition like an authoritarian project. "We have a crisis here, and a crisis is the time for decisive, even dictatorial, leadership. Show complete commitment to agile. There is no turning back. Burn the boats. Get the skeptics out of the way. Install leaders who will relentlessly drive our vision to completion. Let's get these painful changes done so that we and the rest of the organization can get on with running the business." As Luke Skywalker might reply, "Amazing. Every word of what you just said is wrong."

At Bosch Power Tools, Becker's leadership transition helped open him to the possibility of a better way, and the company's adoption of agile gave him a road map. The goals of the transformation that he launched were more innovations that would be of value to users, greater speed and adaptability, and new models for collaboration. He and his six-person transformation team established a vision and set a tone of continuous improvement from the beginning. "This is certainly not a classical project, where everything is defined in detail before it starts," said Anne Kathrin Gebhardt, who led the team. "We are in the middle of an iterative and self-learning process. The path we have chosen is the Bosch Power Tools path. Every company or every business division must define its own path."[7]

After learning from pilot teams, the transformation team began looking at one of the six business units within Power Tools. "A transformation of this nature obviously involves many challenges," said Gebhardt. "After all, it is not merely a simple reorganization, but rather the most far-reaching transformation of our operating system. We are going right back to roots and changing everything, including our management and team culture, our organizational structures, the methodology we employ, and our strategic processes. The key wasn't which topic we dealt with first. Instead, the focus is on addressing every single topic and relating it to a holistic transformation approach." The five tracks of work the transformation team defined were strategy, organization, leadership, processes and methods, and culture. Over three years, the team sequenced through each of the six business units as well as the headquarters functions.

In the leadership track, what was most critical was the time and space for dialogue. For instance, team members sponsored a wide variety of activities—leadership days, training on topics such as coaching and mindfulness, soliciting broad feedback on leadership style to create feedback loops and help leaders, creating more engagement between leadership and front-line teams, and so on. They also began to experiment with agile methodologies and practices in becoming an agile leadership team.

Three years later, agile practices had spread to the entire division. Some innovation cycles moved from three years to six months. Product managers, business owners, and division leaders were holding their stand-ups, reviewing their backlogs, making decisions on the spot wherever possible, and turning out more and more innovations that customers of all sorts would find valuable. As for the financial results, early indicators are encouraging—but time will tell.

FIVE KEY TAKEAWAYS

1. Leaders considering an agile journey should reflect on their leadership style and how they add value. Do they help people to learn by doing? Are they building trust, as opposed to controlling? Are they doing what only they can do, thus capitalizing on their comparative advantage? Are they letting customers speak for themselves as opposed to telling teams what the customer wants?

2. As agile leaders reshape how they add value, they can come together as an agile leadership team. They build the trustworthiness of their teams to run the business. They themselves focus on defining priorities, allocating resources, and removing barriers for teams.

3. An agile leadership team is a critical component of an agile enterprise. Members act as an agile strategy team focused on the greater good rather than their own silos, in order to help the whole

organization succeed. They define their own manifesto to guide their actions.

4. Leaders can change the culture and the organization only if they can change themselves. Leaders who aren't committed to learning and practicing agile methods shouldn't launch an agile transformation.

5. Teams in an agile enterprise must make decisions quickly. Agile leadership teams can support quick decision making by being inclusive, overcommunicating, coaching, and building learning loops.

5

AGILE PLANNING, BUDGETING, AND REVIEWING

No myth about agile is more rampant or ruinous than the claim that agile companies don't have to plan. We meet too many executives who fear adopting agile because of this delusion. We also meet too many agile beginners who try to disguise their failings in planning by arguing that they shouldn't have to plan.

We understand the source of confusion. The agile manifesto states that agile practitioners have come to value "responding to change over following a plan."[1] But that doesn't mean no planning. It means developing *adaptive* plans. Conventional bureaucratic organizations create detailed plans—wasting time and resources in pursuit of precision—and assume that executives will implement them to the letter. Agile practitioners view plans more as testable hypotheses, to be adapted over time. Adaptive planners estimate potential benefits and costs so that people can decide on priorities and budgets. Those are the hypotheses. They also lay out the questions that will determine whether the hypotheses are valid or not. Then they use frequent reviews and empirical data to determine whether to change the plans or change the activities designed to achieve the plan's objectives. Planning, budgeting, and reviewing work together in iterative feedback loops to create an agile plan-do-study-adjust system, just as any individual agile team would.

Improving the agility of planning, budgeting, and reviewing processes is an essential element of creating an agile enterprise. It may improve enterprise agility far more than changing organizational structures or even increasing the number of agile teams. In this chapter we'll look at how companies achieve that objective.

Planning in an Agile Enterprise

In 2014, Dell Inc., as the computer company was then known, was in the midst of a multiyear transformation. The previous December, CEO Michael Dell and an investment firm called Silver Lake Partners had taken the company private. Without the pressure of public earnings releases, Dell could lengthen its innovation horizons. It could accept greater variability in short-term profits in return for greater long-term benefits. But the new strategy would require substantial changes in Dell's then-quite-conventional annual planning cycles.

So Michael Dell decided to implement a new model for strategic planning, budgeting, and reviewing. The firm—known since 2016 as Dell Technologies—now calls it the Dell Management Model. If you were to boil the model down to its essence, it would look something like this: Michael Dell first develops a clear ambition for the company's future value. Company leaders compare this target to a projection of its value on its current trajectory, and they identify the high-level actions required to close the gap between the two. This process produces a multiyear outlook of revenue and profit and a backlog of initiatives. The leaders then develop a detailed one-year operating plan. While this process happens annually, the team challenges the prioritization and resourcing of initiatives periodically during the year, ensuring that Dell can react quickly to changing customer needs, competitor moves, and information about the results of past actions.

Initiatives in this model move through a life cycle. Each begins as an issue or opportunity to be addressed that would help close the gap between the ambition and the status quo projection. Issues and opportunities with the greatest potential impact and organizational breadth are addressed by the company leaders. These initiatives form a backlog called the Dell Agenda. Issues with narrower scope and lesser impact are addressed by the appropriate business unit or function. After each initiative is identified and categorized in one of these groups, it is assigned an owner, provided initial resources for a team, and sequenced in the backlog. Each initiative team then works through a series of steps: gathering facts, developing alternatives, choosing among alternatives, committing to outcomes, gaining approval to execute the initiative, moving forward with the execution, periodically reporting on results, and ultimately being retired as an initiative by being incorporated into Dell's regular operations. Company leaders engage with initiative teams to provide guidance or approvals at various points in this life cycle, typically addressing two or three initiatives from the Dell Agenda each month. The model allows for a great deal of flexibility. Whenever a new issue or opportunity is identified at any time during the year, leaders estimate the rough value at stake. If it's important enough, the opportunity will be added to the Dell Agenda, with an initiative owner assigned, resources allocated, and a place in the sequence established.

An important benefit of the model is focus. The company's leadership team regularly revisits the Dell Agenda and revises it to ensure that it always includes the highest priority issues and opportunities. Because of this review, the agenda typically has fewer than a

dozen active initiatives at any given time. By avoiding the inefficiencies of organizational multitasking, Dell accomplishes much
more each year than would be possible with a less focused approach. Dennis Hoffman, Dell's senior vice president for corporate
strategy, told us, "The Dell Management Model [DMM] ensures
Dell always focuses its resources on the initiatives that will make
the biggest difference to enable our strategic and financial ambitions. Before we started using DMM, we were not always aligned
as an executive leadership team on what the most important issues
were, and it was harder to make progress on issues that cut across
organizational boundaries. Establishing the Dell Agenda has helped
us focus as a leadership team on what matters most, while remain-
ing flexible to adjust as new issues arise. Then we can work together
to achieve our ambition."

Dell uses agile approaches in other ways as well. The company
has focused on improving customer service and cost effectiveness
for many years. For example, leaders in the supply-chain function
wanted to improve their ability to plan demand and supply. In September 2018, Kevin Brown, Dell's chief supply-chain officer, launched
two agile teams staffed with dedicated people from several functions. One team was charged with developing and installing a collaborative planning process with the company's largest customers
to foster an active dialogue around upcoming orders and better
ensure on-time delivery. The team developed process changes, created new tools, and deployed advanced analytical models. But
rather than roll out the new procedures all at once, team members
launched a series of small changes in two-week sprints. Then they
gathered feedback from customers and internal stakeholders and
fine-tuned their solutions. By June 2019 these teams had delivered
multiple solutions that were popular with customers and well received by the internal sales organization. "Since we started using
agile teams about a year ago," said Brown, "we have found the
agile approach to be a differentiated way to drive fast, high-value
change across our operations. The solutions we are developing
using agile methodologies are more innovative, more robust, and

more accepted by our internal and external customers. We're now applying agile values to how we run many of our transformation efforts." At this writing, Dell has scaled up the supply-chain effort to nine teams, expanding the use of agile to continue to improve cost and operational outcomes.

Dell's agile approach to planning has underpinned an ambitious agenda. Since putting the DMM in place five years ago, the company has integrated the largest-ever merger in the technology industry, exited some businesses to transform its portfolio, gained or strengthened leadership positions in several other businesses, improved customer advocacy, reemerged as a public company, and doubled its enterprise value.

As Dell illustrates, agile enterprises tend to do four things differently from conventional companies:

- *They gather extensive customer input.* The planning process is heavily informed by customers, either through direct customer research or by encouraging teams that are closest to customers to suggest elements or improvements.

- *They provide guidance on what to do but leave the how to the agile teams.* In the Dell supply-chain example, functional leaders and agile teams had a great deal of discretion to determine how they would contribute to the company's goals of improved cost effectiveness and on-time delivery.

- *They focus and sequence initiatives to avoid too much multitasking.* Agile enterprises sequence their major initiatives year by year and even quarter by quarter, rather than trying to make some progress on every initiative simultaneously. As we noted, Dell sets a high value hurdle on its corporate initiatives, such that fewer than a dozen are typically active simultaneously.

- *They revisit the plan frequently and make adjustments as needed.* Success in business requires testing strategies by comparing actual outcomes to expected ones and then updating the strategies. That's why Dell creates, refines, assesses, reprioritizes, and sunsets its strategic initiatives throughout the year. The frequent revisiting and updating of plans allows agile enterprises to avoid wasting effort on detailed long-term plans that would likely change many times before they are ever executed.

Agile Budgeting

Budgeting in an agile enterprise serves two main purposes. It provides the controls necessary for the company's operations. It also directs funds to the areas of highest priority for agile innovation. Bureaucratic budgeters typically devote enormous effort to producing precise numbers. Their budgets last for a year or more, meaning that some unproductive projects continue on until their budgets run out. Meanwhile, critical innovation efforts wait in line for the next budget cycle to compete for funding.

Agile budgeters operate with a different mindset and different procedures, particularly where funding innovation is concerned. They recognize that for two-thirds of successful innovations, the original concept will change significantly during the development process. They know that teams will drop some features and launch others without waiting for the next annual cycle. As a result, agile funding procedures often evolve to resemble those of a venture capitalist: the procedures provide opportunities to purchase options for further discovery. Their objective is not to instantly create a large-scale business but, rather, to develop a critical component of the ultimate solution. This leads to a lot of apparent failures but—critically—it accelerates and reduces the cost of learning. Funding decisions look similar in an agile enterprise, greatly improving the speed and efficiency of innovation. Target Corp., for instance, organized its technology to align with its business capabilities and customer experiences. Its more than 250 product managers are like entrepreneurs charged with achieving measurable business results. Those who deliver stronger returns are rewarded with more resources and responsibility.

While most agile enterprises still have an annual budgeting cycle, it is far less onerous than conventional budgeting, and executives update their budgets periodically during the year to reflect both changing conditions and updated information about innovation activities. This flexibility can provide significant benefits. A leading US financial services firm, for instance, offers automobile insurance to its customers. A while ago, it funded several agile teams to develop the elements of a new capability: enabling customers to find cars to buy on its website and mobile app. The company's original idea was to include recommendations about what to buy in addition to the search capability. But when the teams tested the idea, they found that customers valued only the search function, not the recommendations. That changed the group's priorities and allowed one of the teams to be redeployed to other work. In a traditional budgeting environment, the entire project scope would typically have been delivered and the effort to develop the recommendation capability largely wasted.

Agile enterprises typically follow three other practices related to budgeting for innovation:

They Prioritize Strategic Imperatives, but They Also Welcome Unplanned Initiatives

The planning process should clarify strategy and identify the actions required to achieve a company's ambitions. Funding the activities most vital to achieving the strategy should be the highest priority. In some cases those activities may require nearly all the available funding; in others, they may leave substantial room for unpredictable initiatives. So every enterprise needs a prioritized, sequenced backlog of investment opportunities. Backlog items come from a wide variety of sources: the planning process, interesting ideas from ongoing agile teams, new customer research, competitive analysis, suggestions from front-line employees, unexpected acquisition opportunities, and so on. Unplanned initiatives may warrant greater funding than ideas that were once priorities in the planning process but now seem to be flailing or losing relevance.

Amazon Prime and Amazon Web Services, for example, were both ideas generated from the bottom up outside the normal planning cycle. Neither looked like strategic priorities at the time, but they quickly rose in importance as their successful growth required increased funding. Failures at Amazon open up other opportunities. When the Fire Phone fizzled, the company had no shortage of innovative opportunities on its backlog to fund with far better returns. (We'll have more to say about Amazon in chapter 8.)

They Fund Persistent Teams Rather Than Projects When Opportunities Are Enduring

Agile teams come in two types. Project teams address issues or opportunities that can be solved reasonably quickly, typically in weeks or months. Persistent teams (often called product teams) tackle significant customer opportunities that may take years to address properly. As Jeff Bezos likes to say, "Customers are *always* beautifully, wonderfully dissatisfied, even when they report being happy and business is great. Even when they don't yet know it, customers want something better, and your desire to delight customers will drive you to invent on their behalf."[2] As customer needs change and customer solutions evolve, persistent teams will typically pivot dozens of times in a period of years. No one wants teams to come back for approval every time they need to change direction; if they find a better way to offer a customer solution, they should pursue it. (Conversely, if they do not find a good way or the problem is no longer important, the team should move to a different problem or disband.) The longevity and empowerment of persistent agile teams makes them more effective and efficient innovators as they become ever more familiar with one another, with their customers, and with the processes and systems that serve those customers. You can find a deeper treatment of planning, budgeting, and reviewing for persistent teams at the website bain.com/doing-agile-right.

They Tie Funding to Outcomes

Agile enterprises respect results more than seniority. The pet projects of senior leaders are as transparent as any other agile initiative. The opinions of executives are subject to the same scrutiny as those of software engineers: How could we test that?

With funding comes accountability. Every funded agile activity, whether it be a persistent team, a project, a strategic imperative, or an unplanned opportunity, is responsible for delivering the customer outcome that originally justified the investment. This sounds obvious, but it's surprising how many traditional budgeting systems spend months or years deciding whether to invest in a project, then never spend a day determining how the investment actually panned out. Agile budgeting is different. Agile constantly questions whether incremental investments are justified. Agile rewards efficiency in experimentation. Practitioners grow skilled in identifying the most critical questions and devising ingenious ways of formulating prototypes to answer those questions. Agile teams fully expect to find ways to either achieve those outcomes or to pass their budgets on to other agile teams that can create greater value for the money.

Of course, different companies face different challenges. So each develops budgeting procedures that fits its own needs. One example is Royal Bank of Scotland (RBS), a company that you'll read more about in chapter 7. A few years ago, as a core part of an effort to make the bank more customer-focused, leaders in the personal banking division began to create persistent agile teams mapped to specific customer experiences. Unfortunately, RBS's budgeting, funding, and governance model stood in the way. For one thing, the model was designed to fund only traditional projects. It required tremendous detail on features, costs, and outcomes—detail that took a lot of time to prepare and that left teams unable to adapt as they learned more about customer behavior. Because teams were disbanded at the end of each project and reformulated for each new one, teams rarely got the benefits of members working together for a long time. Finally, the approval process for rolling out changes was onerous, which delayed results and made testing and learning from small changes impractical.

So RBS's leaders began reshaping their budgeting and funding model. Step one was to create customer business areas (CBAs) focused on a specific set of experiences, such as home buying and ownership. Step two was to establish persistent journey teams within the CBAs, each one focused on one customer experience, such as disputing a credit card charge. Each CBA has a performance agreement consisting of outcomes such as revenue growth, cost reduction, or Net Promoter Score increase, to which the CBA owner commits in return for the requested resources. Each journey owner is given resources for commitments that support their CBA's performance agreement. This system empowers team members to manage their own backlogs in pursuit of their teams' objectives. Since it was deployed throughout the RBS personal bank, it has reduced the number of business cases developed in a year from eighty to six, which has freed up substantial time and energy. RBS plans to evolve the model further so that funding for CBAs and journey teams is continuously in place and adjusted gradually as customer priorities and business opportunities change.

RBS also uses a technique it calls scenario-based funding to help ensure that it supports the most promising opportunities. It asks business unit heads to provide a base case request for innovation and investment funding and the associated business value that they can deliver. It also asks them to project the incremental value they could deliver with 20 percent more funding and the value that would be lost with 20 percent less. This process allows RBS leaders to consider how shifts in funding among business units could optimize enterprise business value. Business unit leaders develop their estimates and make budget allocation decisions using the same approach with the product leads who report to them.

Agile Reviewing

Reviewing is an essential part of the plan-do-study-adjust cycle. Quarterly, monthly, or even weekly reviews provide frequent opportunities to compare actual versus expected performance, and to determine whether to change plans and budgets or the activities designed to achieve them. But here, too, agile enterprises go about it differently. Participants share information in a transparent and informal way, avoiding the time and effort wasted in preparing slick presentations. They are far more likely to use reviews to update plans and budgets. Their chief goal is to boost rather than hinder the empowerment of agile teams. Reviewers want to give teams the information they need to manage a full range of business considerations, so teams can do their own reviews of topics that, in a bureaucratic organization, would be reviewed by control functions or other managers. This helps avoid excessive top-down direction.

Finance departments, for example, will always manage budgets. But financial managers don't need to keep questioning the decisions of the owners of agile initiatives. "Our CFO constantly shifts accountability to empowered agile teams," says Ahmed Sidky, the head of development management at the videogame company Riot Games. "He'll say, 'I am not here to run the finances of the company. You are, as team leaders. I'm here in an advisory capacity.' In the day-to-day organization, finance partners [are assigned to groups of agile teams]. They don't control what the teams do or don't do. They are more like finance coaches who ask hard questions and provide deep expertise. But ultimately it's the team leader who makes decisions, according to what is best for Riot players."[3]

Riot Games, of course, is a digital-native company with a lot of agile experience. But RBS's personal bank is pursuing a similar goal, adapting its quarterly budget review process to better empower its agile teams. Instead of reviewing project spending and degree of completion versus budget, the quarterly reviews now involve a much more valuable set of discussions revolving around customer business area and journey team performance agreements, including a set of agreed measurable outcomes. Owners report on outcomes achieved and on any that were missed, discussing the reasons and seeking input for improvement. This shift in reviewing focus has contributed to much greater engagement and satisfaction of the owners and their teams. At this writing, the performance agreements of change-the-business innovation teams are separate from those of run-the-business operations teams. But the bank was planning to create a unified set of goals and commitments for both kinds of teams assigned to each customer journey. It was also developing governance changes that should further increase the agility of journey teams. These changes include reducing and accelerating the steps required to approve changes that affect customers and streamlining the reporting of how funds are being used.

Dell—no surprise here—also uses reviews to update plans frequently. Each month, the executive leadership team meeting reviews the results-to-date of some ongoing strategic agenda initiatives. This creates accountability for the initiative owner to deliver promised outcomes. The process avoids the common problem in traditional bureaucracies of projects continuing over many years with little to show for it.

Dell's agile reviewing process also provides information needed for finance's management of the company's annual plan and budget. Finance teams and business-unit leaders develop the annual plan and budget in the fourth quarter of each year, and then they update it twice during the year. The plan and budget include revenue and cost targets by business area, and they reflect the expected impacts of all active initiatives. The process harmonizes innovation and operations teams by having each work toward a shared set of goals. Dell's reviews thus avoid another common problem with traditional bureaucracies: their difficulty in adjusting annual budgets to reflect the impact of changing conditions.

———————

The right cadence for the planning, budgeting, and reviewing cycle depends on the organization, and particularly on where the balance lies between stability and innovation. Too slow a cycle can lead to stagnation or misdirected resources. Too fast a cycle can create unnecessary work and confusion in operations. Most agile enterprises find that the right balance is to update corporate and business unit plans and budgets at least every few months and at most every month.

The transition from conventional planning, budgeting, and reviewing to agile will initially feel risky to control-oriented executives. It goes to the heart of a company's financial control, which is a fundamental responsibility of the chief executive, the CFO, and the board. It raises questions about the traditional mechanisms for planning work and allocating resources. It also involves power shifts at every level of management as agile teams take on more responsibility and decision-making authority. Making these changes throughout a large corporation all at once can indeed be risky. But the use of agile principles reduces the risk significantly. Companies that succeed at such a transition make a point of laying out the failings of existing processes and showing how the new model can overcome them. They connect the CFO and other senior leaders to other firms that have successfully made the transition. They pilot the new plan-budget-review model to prove its benefits and then roll it out incrementally, perhaps by business unit or geography.

However they may make the journey to agile planning, budgeting, and reviewing, it is an essential one for any company aspiring to be an agile enterprise.

FIVE KEY TAKEAWAYS

1. Contrary to popular myth, planning is an essential part of agile. Planning, budgeting, and reviewing must work together in frequent, adaptive cycles.

2. Best practices for agile planning include gathering extensive bottom-up input, planning only as much and as soon as needed, prioritizing and sequencing initiatives to minimize work in process and multitasking, and revising plans in light of new information.

3. Best practices for budgeting include prioritizing strategic imperatives while welcoming attractive unplanned initiatives, funding persistent agile teams for enduring opportunities, and using a venture capital approach that flexibly adjusts budgets based on results.

4. Best practices for reviewing include frequent transparent, informal opportunities to compare actual versus expected performance and determine whether to change plans and budgets or to change the activities for achieving them.

5. While changing the planning, budgeting, and reviewing process may seem risky to control-oriented executives, it is actually one of the easier steps on the road to becoming an agile enterprise. The change can be navigated successfully with an agile approach, including proving the new model through pilots and executing a phased rollout.

6

AGILE
ORGANIZATION,
STRUCTURES,
AND PEOPLE
MANAGEMENT

Creating an agile enterprise nearly always involves changes in a company's operating model and in all that the operating model entails. Roles and responsibilities need to be redefined and decision rights adjusted. Core management practices and procedures must be refined. Talent management practices have to be reconsidered and basic ways of working overhauled. Organizational structures must often be reshaped as well. Unless leaders decide to change everything at once—seldom the best option—they must figure out how to sequence and test all these changes in good agile fashion. It's a tall order. People who are accustomed to bureaucratic methods—most leaders, in other words—often find themselves tempted to look for a shortcut.

The most common temptation, without a doubt, is to redo the company's structure and stop there. It seems so easy! You can reshape the org chart just by moving around the boxes and reporting lines. Restructuring lets you remove people and costs. It lets you fill important roles with individuals who are supportive of the change you have in mind. If you change the jobs, you might think, you will force changes in how people approach their work. Changing the ways of working, in turn, will change outputs and outcomes. Presto: an agile enterprise.

A related temptation is copying. We have mentioned the danger of copying earlier in this book, but it's particularly germane to the question of organization because you can actually look at some other company's org chart and take that as a guideline. So let's examine the org chart of Spotify, the Sweden-based music-streaming company that is probably the most frequently emulated agile organizational model of all (figure 6-1).

As you inspect the illustration, you may be surprised. It probably looks a great deal like your own company's org chart, and indeed like the org chart of nearly any traditionally organized enterprise. Of course, if you were to dig down deeper, you would find a lot of *squads* and *tribes* and *chapters* and *guilds*, all relatively unfamiliar terminology. But most of these agile teams and other groupings are embedded within Spotify's R&D function. Other people, those in the operations and support and control functions, are organized into traditional departments. R&D does account for about half the employees of this digital-native company. In other companies, however, the proportion of employees focused on agile innovation may be only 10 or 15 percent.

We offer these observations to introduce three points:

- An organization's operating model should not be confused with its formal structure—it includes accountabilities and decision rights, a management system, leadership behaviors, culture, collaboration methodologies, and so on, in addition

FIGURE 6-1

Spotify organization chart

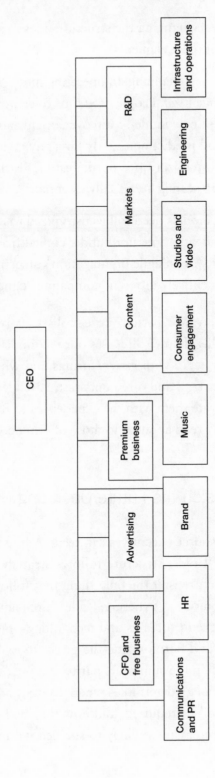

Source: "Spotify," The Official Board, https://www.theofficialboard.com/org-chart/spotify (accessed January 22, 2020).

to structure. Changing the structure doesn't automatically alter any of these elements.

- The process of changing an operating model is as important as the change itself. People need time to create—and get accustomed to—a new model. Moreover, organizations are complex systems, and predicting exactly how any given change will affect the organization is hard. Testing, learning, and step-by-step scaling are usually essential.

- Operating models need to be customized to each company's strategy and situation, not blindly copied from someone else. Lifting parts of an agile organization's structure and applying them to an entirely different company is dangerous.

Fortunately, there are better, more holistic ways to change an organization. This chapter discusses our recommendations, such as why we seldom begin with restructurings and why tuning the talent engine is a critical and often underestimated lever in the transition. We'll illustrate them with the experiences of Bosch, a company you have already read about, and those of other companies as well.

Envision the Future Operating Model

Most human resource executives can recite Alfred D. Chandler Jr.'s famous quote: "Unless structure follows strategy, inefficiency results."[1] But structure isn't the only thing that follows strategy. The entire operating model—structure; leadership; planning, budgeting, and reviewing; even processes and technology—must follow strategy, integrating and harmonizing the pieces to make the company more valuable than the sum of its parts.

Corporate strategy determines where to play, how to win, what business units will be required, and how they will operate. For example, is our strategy most likely to succeed with centralized divisions, decentralized business units, or a matrix organization that tries to capture the benefits of both scale and autonomy? Once these decisions are made, two more become critical: How many business units should we have, and how should we define them so that business unit leaders have the authority to quickly make tough trade-offs without causing problems for other performance units? Define business units correctly and you create highly empowered leaders who take full ownership for delivering results. Define them incorrectly and you create intracompany overlaps and chaos.

To define business units, executives often use simplifying shortcuts and mathematical clustering techniques. Calculate the amount of cost sharing among operating units. Determine their potential to share capabilities. Measure the overlaps in current customer purchasing patterns. If these quantifications yield high numbers, then combine the operations into a single business unit. If not, separate them. These techniques can yield quick insights into effective business definitions in current market conditions. But the work isn't finished until you work backward from customer needs. Business units exist to satisfy customer needs profitably, not to crank out products. Printed encyclopedias and Wikipedia are in the same business, even if their cost structures and manufacturing processes are quite different. The same is true of incandescent light bulbs and light emitting diodes (LEDs). Business definition and matrix choices that give a company an advantage in meeting today's customer needs must not impede its ability to change how it meets customer needs in the future.

Bad business definition is a leading cause of rising business mortality rates. Physical retailers get destroyed by Amazon. Chemical photography is ravaged by digital cameras. Typewriters are wiped out by word processors. Video rental companies are bankrupted by video streaming. These are all because too many businesses define their boundaries by how they make products instead of why customers buy them. Then, suddenly, new competitors seem to come out of nowhere. There is no cost sharing with current products. The innovations require entirely new capabilities. And some of the customers that buy these new products aren't even current customers. In order for business units to both run the business and change the business in such turbulent times, they must be defined in ways that proactively encourage them to continuously adapt to changing customer needs.

Agile teams can provide that adaptation, and proper business definition should guide where they are placed and how they are used. Placing agile teams within the right business units improves the odds that their innovative work will be adopted and scaled quickly and effectively. Ensuring that agile teams do not break the business unit into fragments that destroy responsibility and accountability improves performance. Giving agile teams customer-oriented missions helps leaders to change their businesses with—or even in advance of—changing customer needs.

When executives do this correctly, they create a structure that looks something like figure 6-2. Agile innovation teams will be spread throughout the company. Except for disruptive innovations that fall outside of existing business units or across several of them, agile teams will be located as close as possible to the operations that must adopt and scale them. This recommendation runs contrary to many scaling models, which prefer to pull the teams away from operations and cluster them together in large tribes. But there are good reasons for business owners to own agile teams whenever possible. First, the best leaders are change oriented. When accountability for change is removed from a business unit, the move takes away a leader's vision, creativity, and inspiration. He or she is no longer leading the business into the future. Companies that want high-performing leaders need to empower them and design accountabilities that let them lead. Second, generating creative ideas is not usually the hardest part of successful innovation. Scaling is. Building a prototype is relatively easy compared to profitably scaling that prototype across the business. Unless line managers own innovative solutions, those solutions will lie fallow inside the snazziest of innovation labs.

FIGURE 6-2

What might the structure of an agile enterprise look like?

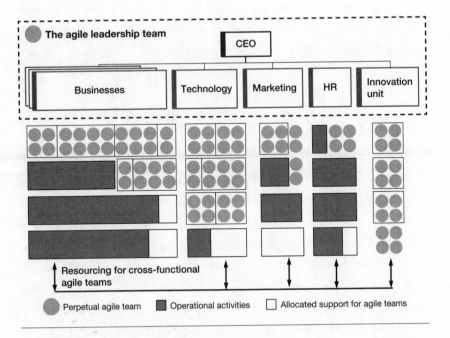

An organization's structure is the easiest part to illustrate, but it's important for companies to sketch out their entire operating model. How will decision rights work? Who sets budget levels? Where is an employee's home base? Who handles recruiting, training, performance reviews, compensation, promotions, and career tracks? Which functions should be centralized shared services versus decentralized operations? How are cost allocations determined? Can business units decide to purchase shared services from outsider third parties? Can shared services sell their services to outsider third parties? No structure will ever be perfect. The good news is that it doesn't need to be. By intelligently mixing all the elements of the operating model, executives can ensure that no single element constrains success. A structure change may not be needed—or else it can be significantly delayed in order to focus on changes in areas such as decision rights, leadership, and ways of working. Forming agile teams may not even require changing reporting lines for employees. Agile team members would still report to their home departments, but their managers would act as long-term professional development coaches rather than as day-to-day supervisors. Daily activities would be planned and executed with the teams.

Figure Out How—and How Fast—to Get There

A company embarking on an agile transformation has a built-in advantage over companies seeking other kinds of changes, because it has the tools of agile at its disposal. It naturally has to ask how far it wants to go, how fast, where to start, and how to sequence the changes. If its leaders are familiar with agile principles (and we hope by now that they are), they will understand that the appropriate sequence is test, learn, and scale. They will also understand that they must engage the organization in the process, designing and cocreating changes to test with people from every discipline and level of the company—no closed doors. At each phase, the design process will need to clarify what work is to be done by which group and who will be responsible for each key decision. Agile works best when decisions are pushed down the organization as far as possible, so long as people have appropriate guidelines and expectations about when to escalate a decision to a higher level.

The company also needs to take into account the entire landscape of proposed changes in the operating model: not just structure but changes in accountabilities and decision rights, in the management system, in leadership, and so on. It can speed up or slow down based on how things are working out. Companies that move with deliberate speed to create pull from other teams generally achieve better business results than those that try to move as fast as they possibly can. The latter group usually find themselves creating disruption in the organization without any obvious benefit, thereby undermining their claims for the future.

Bosch Power Tools offers an almost textbook case of these precepts. The division took a carefully sequenced, multiyear approach to becoming an agile enterprise. The first pilot teams were in the home and garden business unit. After learning from the pilots for about six months, leaders began expanding the number of teams until they eventually encompassed the entire unit. The division then began transforming its other five business units in sequence over a two-year period. At this writing, Power Tools is focusing on how to improve the support and control functions, such as finance, HR, and logistics.

At the outset, the division established five pillars to guide its transformation: strategy, organization, leadership, processes and methods, and culture. As each new business unit began the process, volunteers from every level and department staffed temporary project teams to design the new organization. The discussions were wholly transparent, and the teams used an iterative process to incorporate feedback and adapt accordingly. In one unit, the team responsible for organization structure used Lego blocks of different colors to represent various disciplines. The exercise allowed team members to discuss and test how people would be deployed under different alternatives. Building a prototype was much more powerful and inspiring than drawing boxes and lines on paper.

Over time, the leaders of Power Tools learned from their experience and adjusted their approach. By the time they launched the third business unit, for instance, they were spending the first two months on the *why*, so that people would understand the reasoning behind the transformation. And although they focused on structure during the first year of the process, they concluded after a year that collaboration and culture required more emphasis. Ways of working were more important and represented a bigger change than the structure alone. Leaders also significantly increased their focus on supporting new leadership behaviors, holding leadership days across the enterprise. And they made significant investments in learning. Depending on their positions, some people might attend a leadership academy while others attended functional academies. Employees received focused feedback and coaching. They learned agile basics, design thinking, and mindfulness. Having agile coaches in place early on helped each business unit understand the new approaches and drive productivity improvements.

Power Tools did undergo a sizable change in structure, and company leaders view it as a key enabler of the agile transformation. The new structure broke down functional silos, created smaller P&L units, and reduced the levels of hierarchy from five to three. But the company made the change carefully, piloting it first and then implementing it over three years. Also, structure was just one of several tracks, and in fact the bigger impact may have been on ways of working. Over time, the division created fifty-five business teams with end-to-end accountability and decision rights, even including manufacturing. This change, combined with the agile leadership process described in chapter 4, sped up decision making. The teams were close to their units' operations, which allowed for faster response times when issues cropped up. Decisions that once went up the manufacturing silo and then over to other relevant silos could now be made on the spot. "We all belong to one purpose team," said Daniela Kraemer, a business owner in light drilling and chiseling. "For instance, we have a plant in China. People at the plant detected a problem with a supplier, involving the switching elements, and stopped production. That same day, we took countermeasures, and the sales and marketing teams communicated with customers. We could not have been faster. We were solving the problem together."[2]

Building a Talent Engine

"I wish our company had started work on talent earlier." We can scarcely count the number of times we have heard that regret from executives whose companies are launching agile. Conversely, companies that gave HR leaders a seat at the table right at the beginning—and then asked those individuals to lead the way in talent development—found that their transformation process sped up immeasurably.

Why so? In any company, business strategy informs talent strategy. The company's strategic and operational requirements determine not just the kind of people it needs but also what those people can reasonably expect and aspire to. Oddly, many companies don't do the kind of workforce planning that this linkage implies. They may not assess the talent implications of a new business strategy. They may not figure out what sorts of people they need, how many, where those people should work, and whether they should be accessed through partners.

An agile transformation can't succeed without this kind of planning. Agile almost by definition requires specific new skills and hence new talent. HR leaders at nearly every company will discover right away that there are gaps in the workforce, particularly in critical in-house technology disciplines. As they begin to dedicate resources to projects, they will likely find gaps in specialized areas of expertise. In the past, the experts might have been shared across a dozen projects; in an agile environment, that is not an option. A company is also likely to find that it must carry a bench for some capabilities—that is, whenever the cost of carrying a bench is less than the potential cost of not having the necessary skills. The good news is that agile itself can be helpful here. For example, HR managers can prototype workforce planning improvements for one bottlenecked resource in one part of the business. Then they can learn from that experience and scale the planning accordingly.

In some situations, HR may find that it is cheaper and easier to train people in new skills than to find talent externally. A hire and fire approach is expensive with severance cost, recruitment cost, and joining incentives. Most of the time, indeed, the vast majority of people who will be working in an agile enterprise are the people who are in the organization today. That is an asset, not a liability. After all, you need people who have experience dealing with your customers and who understand what they value. You need people who understand how your operations and processes and systems work. People trained in agile aren't particularly distinctive. People who know how agile might work in your organization are. Anyway, many of these people will not be using agile methodologies directly. Operations teams will need to know what the transition means for them; they may be involved with agile teams and may have to learn new skills, such as participating in testing and scaling. But most will not be on agile teams, and so will need only to adopt agile values rather than agile methods.

The Talent System

Talent strategy informs a company's talent system, meaning the processes it relies on to acquire, develop, deploy, manage, and reward its people. Several aspects of this system will have to be revamped as part of an agile transformation. Senior leaders and HR staff will need to figure out how each one should evolve—including the HR department itself. An example may help to show some of what's involved.

Walmart has more than a million associates. So Julie Murphy, the company's chief people officer for the United States, has a lot of customers, and she is responsible for improving their experience. To do so, she studies the different segments of her customer base and tries to understand both their overall journey and key episodes in it. She and her team define their priorities based on the importance, the frequency, and the opportunity for improvement in the various episodes.

In early 2018, Murphy established five agile teams based on these priorities to accelerate the pace of innovation. The teams focused on hiring, learning, progression, performance management, and simplification. Changing to agile teams brought more transparency to the work. It improved the group's ability to set priorities. And indeed, the pace of innovation increased dramatically. One team, for instance, focused on the hiring of front-line associates. The group working on this experience—which included fully dedicated members with expertise in HR and tech—developed a tool to better assess potential candidates, reduce bias in the hiring process, and decrease the administrative burden for everyone.

The team's first release provided field HR reps with a prioritized list of candidates, powered by an algorithm in the background that aggregated and analyzed more than twenty data points. Team members launched the tool in one market, captured feedback from store managers and HR people in the field, and then launched a second release in a different market for more testing and learning. By mid-2019, the new tool—dubbed Hiring Helper—was showing a 20 percent improvement in hiring fit compared to traditional selection methods. In addition, candidates selected using the tool showed a 5 percent decrease in attrition and a 15 to 30 percent decrease in absenteeism in the first two releases. At this writing, the team was continuing to test, learn, and scale.

Walmart, of course, is just one company. The number of agile teams other companies require in the HR domain will vary based on the magnitude and scope of the changes needed to support the agile transformation. Simple HR policies or practice changes may be straightforward to implement. Bigger process and technology innovations may benefit from agile teaming. Let's discuss some of the principles guiding these changes.

Foster Leadership, Not Just Management

Leadership means more than simply being in charge of a group and delivering the desired outcomes. Agile leaders in particular should be rewarded on how they contribute to an agile environment. In one area of Bosch Power Tools, for instance, leaders asked a group of more than fifty people to define a set of leadership attributes—skills and characteristics that would be used to assess candidates for advancement. The group defined five criteria: observation, empathy, heart, autonomy, and adaptability. In short, it wasn't enough for someone to produce great results; he or she also had to be the right kind of leader. The division also moved away from a boss-nominated process to a self-nominated process in which a committee judges the candidates. The new system mitigated the common situation in which managers move from one assignment to another and never stay with one boss long enough for that boss to nominate them for advancement.

Agile enterprises also emphasize coaching over career paths; there is no longer one road to the top. Employees in an agile enterprise can learn, take on big opportunities, and make themselves more valuable without getting promoted. In more of a choose-your-own-adventure world, many companies are shifting career development to the individual and providing coaching support. These companies are also supporting leaders in building coaching skills. At Bosch, coaching was a key theme of the learning program for the agile transformation, and it extended beyond the agile teams and into operations. One plant manager in China was so inspired by the learning that he invested his personal time in becoming a certified coach.

Bring in New Talent Inspired by Your Mission

Agile companies focus their talent acquisition approach on mission and results rather than on status or a glossy résumé. Stripe, a digital payments company, leads with its mission in describing how candidates will have an "unprecedented opportunity to put the global economy within everyone's reach while doing the most important work of your career."[3] Stripe uses few titles. It warns candidates, "After a few years your LinkedIn might not look as tricked-out as your peers' at other companies."[4] As a result, it attracts people who are comfortable in the company's culture and agile environment. And it isn't just the cultural benefit. The research reported by our colleagues Michael Mankins and Eric Garton in their book *Time, Talent, Energy* suggests that inspired employees boost productivity.[5]

People can be inspired by the company mission, by their immediate supervisor, or by participation in a productive agile team.

Focus Performance Management on Improvement

Agile teams set clear goals for themselves. They try to understand what goes well and what doesn't go well as they pursue those goals. Feedback should encourage this learning, with the objective of improving results in the future. It should not be all about compensation. When performance management focuses too much on rewards, the discussion changes: superiors may feel constrained about what kind of feedback they offer if they know it will change someone's compensation. Bosch Power Tools used to give employees feedback once a year at an annual performance review, just as many companies do. As the division evolved into an agile enterprise, people developed tools that allowed regular feedback to each team. "That feedback is leading to flexible changes of behavior and attitude," division CEO Henk Becker told us.[6]

Enable Dynamic Resourcing and Attractive Career Paths

Agile companies simplify their job architecture—titles, levels, and pay grades—particularly in the disciplines that are most likely to provide members for agile teams. So some companies may also need to develop expert tracks. Teams need to be able to easily describe the resources they need and take part in selection. "Before, HR was involved and the boss was involved," said Becker. "Now we have team staffing, with involvement across disciplines and hierarchy. The team should have a vote on whether they want this kind of boss, regarding competence and personality."[7]

Employees need to be able to grow without moving up a layer, and their titles should make sense throughout the enterprise. At Bosch Power Tools, said Becker, "The career path is different. We have expertise roles, excellence roles, business owners. We created new roles, which gave people the possibility of forming a T-shaped profile, competence where they are deep but also the top of the T where they work on the complete value chain." Becoming an agile master (Scrum master) is also a new development opportunity at Bosch.

Provide Tools for Team Effectiveness

Bosch Power Tools was experimenting with a variety of managerial tools to help teams be more successful. The division had a tool called individual development discussions (IDD), for example, through which an employee could invite coworkers to provide feedback. In the past, the input would have come from people in other areas or disciplines. Now, some teams were using the process to gather input from those whom they worked with every day. "People are more and more starting to ask for feedback," said Anne Lis, an HR specialist with the division.[8] Power Tools was also sponsoring team target workshops, in which a team meets together and defines collective targets based on input from leaders on financial expectations. Members define the competencies they need to reach those targets and determine what they need to do to attain them. The sessions may be moderated by an agile master, by someone from HR, or by a team member.

Reward Teaming

Companies can think about rewards at four different levels: the individual, the team, the team of teams, and the enterprise. Agile companies focus their rewards both on the value individuals bring to the organization and on the collective success of the teams those individuals are a part of. Base compensation may be market driven, but incentive compensation nearly always has to be based on team or enterprise outcomes. As people advance and take on more responsibility, the proportion of enterprise-based rewards increases.

More junior employees may be compensated on individual and team outcomes while senior employees are compensated on a mix of individual, team of teams, and enterprise results. Of course, rewards should always be viewed in context: they must be based on the culture, values, and behaviors that the company is trying to encourage.

Microsoft's infamous approach to performance management and rewards in the early 2000s offers a cautionary tale. For many years, the software giant used a stack ranking system as part of its performance evaluation model. At regular intervals, report Mankins and Garton, "a certain percentage of any team's members would be rated 'excellent,' 'good,' 'average,' 'below average,' or 'poor,' regardless of the team's overall performance."[9] Since compensation was directly tied to each employee's performance rating, exceptionally talented people avoided teaming with other exceptional players, because it would risk undermining their performance rating and compensation. In effect, the internal market system discouraged teamwork, with predictable effects on productivity. "It took just 600 Apple engineers less than two years to develop, debug, and deploy OS X, a revolutionary change in the company's operating system. By contrast, it took as many as 10,000 engineers more than five years to develop, debug, deploy, and eventually retract Microsoft's Windows Vista."[10] At least a portion of this fortyfold difference in productivity can be explained by Apple's emphasis on team-based rewards and Microsoft's use of individually based stack ranking.

———————

There is a lot to consider in designing a holistic operating model—integrating your organization structure, accountabilities and decision rights, the management system, ways of working, talent practices, and so on. When you do it well, you create mission-inspired teams that work together across the organization, both the run-the-business and the change-the-business elements. You won't have all of the answers at the beginning. That is OK. You are not supposed to.

FIVE KEY TAKEAWAYS

1. How an organization works holistically—its operating model—is significantly more important than its formal structure alone. You need more than structural change to break down silos and hierarchies.

2. Envision the future operating model with proper business definition to design business units and P&Ls that make strategic sense. Agile teams will be dispersed throughout the organization. It's typically more important to locate teams close to where their innovations will be applied than to locate them close to other agile teams.

3. Pace yourself to create pull and build momentum. The sequenced plan needs to include all the elements of the operating model—accountabilities and decision rights, management system, leadership and culture, talent practices, and the like.

4. Continuously revisit your talent strategy, recognizing that while you will need some new talent, most of the people in your future organization are already there. That's a good thing.

5. A company's talent system requires a significant amount of work; get started early and make HR a critical partner in the change.

7

AGILE PROCESSES AND TECHNOLOGY

When Ross McEwan became CEO of Royal Bank of Scotland (RBS) in late 2013, he mapped out a bold agenda. Henceforth, serving customers well would be RBS's core purpose. The bank would aim to be number one in the industry for customer service, trust, and advocacy. Its core values—such as working together as one team and always behaving with integrity—would support and reflect this ambition. A few months later, McEwan appointed Les Matheson CEO of RBS's Personal and Business Banking division. Over the next three years, Matheson would build the bank's home mortgage business into one of the top three in the United Kingdom, while also improving its customer service, customer advocacy, and cost position.

By then, however, the business was facing stronger headwinds. Market demand was down. So were margins. New, technology-savvy competitors were springing up, including fast-growing digital brokers such as Trussle and fintech firms such as Habito. To meet these challenges and open new growth opportunities, Matheson turned first to RBS's core purpose: serving customers well. Mortgage customers, he saw, would be better served if the bank could change its traditional mortgage business into a digital home buying and ownership business based on high-quality customer experience.

Matheson's strong belief that a business will be most successful by finding ways to best serve customers' underlying needs went back to his first job. He began his career at Procter & Gamble in brand management, where understanding and delivering for customers was at the heart of the enterprise. But in his quest to create a digital home ownership business, he faced three major stumbling blocks. One was the budgeting process we discussed in chapter 5. Another barrier, also touched on in chapter 5, was an organizational structure based more on internal considerations, such as financial products, than on customer-related considerations. The third stumbling block was RBS's inflexible procedures, systems, and data. Matheson had been trying for years, for example, to replace the bank's cumbersome mortgage application, which averaged sixty-six pages of paper, with a paperless application. The innovation required process changes in several different departments, most of which were unaccustomed to working in concert. It also required changes in a range of systems with many competing demands for software development resources. Compounding these difficulties was a siloed way of working among the business, IT, and the change organization.

Matheson understood that he couldn't achieve his vision if everyone continued to operate in the same way. Most fundamentally, he felt the bank had to shift its approach from developing and selling financial products to serving customers' financial needs. He began by assembling seven small cross-functional teams to focus on seven journeys, each one addressing a customer need. These included large, complex journeys such as "get a mortgage," midsize ones such as "report and manage fraud," and small ones such as "replace a debit card." Matheson learned two important things by watching these teams work. First, he saw that the journeys related to home buying and ownership appeared to have the greatest potential for providing more value to customers, so he decided to focus there initially. Second, he realized that simply putting together cross-functional teams and giving them a mission wasn't enough. He had been hearing for some time about agile innovation from colleagues inside and outside the bank, and realized that a broader set of agile practices could make the teams more effective and better sustain their success. After learning more, he decided to embark on a customer-focused agile transformation, beginning with the home mortgage business.

The leadership team Matheson established to pursue this goal began its work. Team members first used the methods known as human-centered design to develop a customer-focused North Star—a vision of what experiences and benefits customers value most from financial services providers—to guide the innovation activities. In interviews, company representatives spelled out two elements of the North Star: "I see the bank as the gateway that connects me to the experts and tools I need" and "The bank makes it easier for me to find, buy, and manage my home digitally, with help when I need it."[1]

Next, the team developed a structure that included every key customer experience and the business objectives for each one. The home mortgage application was one such experience; its objectives included dramatically reducing the time and effort required for a customer to complete the application and for the bank to approve it. Then the leadership group began to populate dedicated, cross-functional agile teams mapped to these experiences. It also put in place a variety of enablers to allow the teams to innovate rapidly. For example, team members were colocated, and their funding was tied to business outcomes rather than to product features. "Organizing around customer journeys is at the heart of our new model," Matheson told us. "This construct uniquely allows a cross-functional team to take the customer point of view in every interaction with the bank. Try as we might, we could never accomplish that with our old financial-product-focused, functional organization."[2]

The agile leadership team, headed by Frans Woelders, the retail bank's chief digital officer, knew it needed to deliver impressive wins to build momentum for the agile transition. They decided to focus first on only one or two of the biggest opportunities that the business units and innovation teams passionately believed they could accomplish. The mortgage application experience was to be the province of one of the earliest persistent customer journey teams, as the agile groups were known. In the design vision, the application could be completed on a smartphone or computer in less than an hour. The follow-up discussion (for regulatory purposes) would take place on the phone rather than in person, and the bank would give the applicant a decision in a few days rather than in weeks.

Led by the designers, people on the team conducted customer research to gather feedback. Team members with operations and customer service backgrounds then designed new digital and people-based processes to create the experience that customers wanted, and the team's software engineers wrote the code to enable these new processes, assisted by data engineers and data analysts who ensured the availability and maintenance of accurate data. Members accomplished all these steps in two-week sprints with customer feedback at the end of each one. Initially, customers saw a partial prototype. Then they saw full prototypes and finally complete production systems. Agile team members from operations led the training of loan application advisors in the new processes, first with a small group when the new application was in limited release, and then with the full group of advisors prior to general release. "Having the business and technology people work together as one team is essential to success," Woelders said to us. "Having these groups work separately, even with the best efforts at alignment, would not have given us anything close to the speed and product quality we require. Starting with home buying and ownership, we have now engaged in the new ways of working across all customer business areas."[3]

To allow the mortgage application team and the other journey teams to achieve this level of success and speed, RBS installed several other agile enablers. It implemented the budgeting, funding, and governance changes we discussed in chapter 5. It added team-based performance measures. It put in place select practices from the Scaled Agile Framework—one of the scaling frameworks discussed in chapter 2—to manage the interdependencies between core systems and the many journey teams that these systems serviced.

As the organization's agile capabilities improved, so did results. Adopting agile allowed the personal bank's home buying and ownership business to radically increase the pace of innovation. The bank launched the United Kingdom's first paperless mortgage application; now 90 percent of all applications are paperless. It increased mortgage switching via digital channels from 34 percent in the first half of 2017 to about 60 percent a year later. It reduced average application-to-offer time from twenty-three days to eleven. These innovations helped RBS achieve market-leading Net Promoter scores from customers taking out a new mortgage. At this writing, the mortgage application team is staying in place and will strive to continue improving the process over time. The goal is to reduce customer effort and approval time still further and, of course, to stay ahead of increasingly capable competitors. Meanwhile, success in the home buying and ownership business has helped build the broader organization's commitment to agile ways of working, leading to the rollout of agile across the entire personal bank.

The Challenge of Processes and Technology

By this point in the book, you should have a good idea of how agile can help companies design great customer solutions, meaning the products and services that provide consumers or business buyers with the value they seek. But every service and every product depends upon processes, the steps and procedures by which companies create and deliver those products. The processes, in turn, are nearly always underpinned by technology, primarily software.

Yet for most companies, existing processes and technology are barriers to great customer solutions, not enablers. Think about RBS's starting point: its cumbersome processes and systems got in the way of delivering a great service. It's a common situation. For example, a company's regional offices or business units might be doing things very differently from one another, making integration and training difficult or impossible. Nobody did that on purpose; it was just the result of thousands of small decisions over the years being made by different people. Or perhaps a company made a series of acquisitions and never effectively integrated them, leaving a host of different and less-than-optimal systems in place. Again, the processes and technology that company employees then have to deal with are apt to engender frustration and inefficiencies.

Sad to say, IT departments and the software they develop are notorious for creating such difficulties. A common issue for some companies is spending millions on customized software when standard off-the-shelf solutions would meet their needs. They develop their software through the traditional waterfall process, with every requirement spelled out in advance and the software inevitably loaded up with features that nobody uses. They thereby create a level of complexity that mere human beings can't easily cope with. Many IT departments get so backed up with requests for changes or for new products that a sort of shadow IT emerges: executives fed up with waiting create mini–IT departments of their own or seek out external providers. This, of course, only worsens the complexity, creating unnecessarily diverse processes, systems, and technical standards.

Bureaucracies, being bureaucracies, typically stick with the processes and technology they have in place for as long as they possibly can, which in most cases is far too long. Changing them, after all, is going to be expensive. The changes are going to get in the way of day-to-day business. And the results probably won't be that much

FIGURE 7-1

The taxonomy of opportunities aligns three components

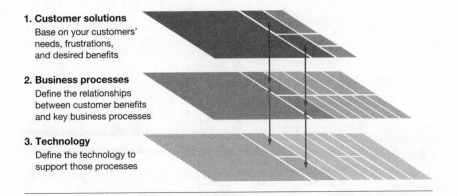

1. **Customer solutions**
   Base on your customers' needs, frustrations, and desired benefits

2. **Business processes**
   Define the relationships between customer benefits and key business processes

3. **Technology**
   Define the technology to support those processes

better anyway—or at least such is the bureaucratic mindset. When things get too bad or too costly, of course, the senior team will finally decide that it's time for a change. They go behind closed doors, decide the specs and the budget for the new processes and systems, and then tell their underlings to work it all out. These organizations are chronically unbalanced, alternating between stagnation and occasional fits of ineffective change.

As we saw with RBS, companies pursuing the agile journey go about things differently. They understand that customer solutions should be driven by customer needs. They understand that these solutions should shape processes and that technology should support and automate these processes (see figure 7-1). Agile practitioners also know that solutions, processes, and technology must continually adapt as customer needs change. They believe that agile teams are the tools best suited to develop innovative solutions when what to deliver, how to deliver it, or both, are vague and unpredictable—the typical situation when addressing customer needs. They know that innovation and operations teams must collaborate closely and in some cases should even be merged.

In this chapter we'll explore innovations in processes and technology and see how they support the creation of industry-leading customer solutions. The chapter primarily addresses processes and systems that underlie service-related customer solutions rather than physical products—but this does include the many services that support physical products.

Working Backward from Customer Solutions

Solution teams innovating processes and technology need to focus on customers, just like any other agile team. Sometimes the relevant customers will be internal. But even then it's important to consider the needs of the external customers being served by those internal customers. Too often, functions such as IT and finance still reflexively focus inward rather than on the needs of the customers they serve—one reason for the bad rap of many IT departments. Innovations in these areas too often reflect what software engineers or finance specialists think is important rather than what their customers might find most valuable. Agile teams that are changing processes and systems, by contrast, treat customer solution, process, and technology innovations as agile products. Working from the customer backward, their goal is to ensure that all these innovations meet customer needs as simply and effectively as possible.

The starting point should always be the solution—the creation of a particular customer experience, such as applying for a mortgage, or the development of a certain capability, such as verifying customers' stated incomes and assets. Usually, customer experience is the better tool for solution definition, because it's typically easiest to link what customers experience with what they value. But capability is the better construct in some situations, such as when a capability underpins many different experiences or when organizing by experience is impractical. Both experiences and capabilities often cut across functional and departmental boundaries, so the most effective teams will draw from all the units that are affected. When solutions are large enough to span more than one team, a company can break the solutions into modular components. That way, each team can test options with customers and proceed relatively independently, giving all the teams the greatest possible control and speed.

In chapter 2, we discussed the benefits of structuring agile teams around a taxonomy of related solutions. This holds true for the customer solutions that drive processes and technology. For instance, a leading US health insurance company developed a taxonomy based on five portfolios: plan members, employers, healthcare providers, benefits brokers, and employees. Each of five portfolio owners acts as the chief product manager for the full set of experiences and capabilities serving that portfolio. A few capabilities, such as claims processing, cut across multiple portfolios and are led by a chief capability owner. This kind of structure allows the company to create road maps for larger solutions that require teams of teams, and it helps manage interdependencies among those teams.

Changes in customer solutions, processes, and technology are highly interdependent, so a team responsible for innovation in any of these areas is frequently empowered to change all three. If that task is too big for one team, multiple teams coordinate closely. Moreover, as we discussed in chapter 5, most companies find that persistent teams are more effective than project teams for solution innovation.

Learning from experiments is fundamental to agile innovation. But experimenting with innovations in customer solutions underpinned by processes and technology presents some specific challenges. Bureaucracies strive for clear, stable, predictable operations. Most traditional operations groups aren't set up to make small, frequent process changes. It's the same for traditional IT groups— they can't easily make small, frequent changes in their systems' functionality. Larger issues intrude as well. Many companies, especially in regulated industries, have lengthy and elaborate procedures that must be followed before anyone can alter processes or technology. Many lack the analytic and technical skills required to design tests and measure outcomes in a manner that maximizes learning. Executives and managers frequently express concern that failed tests will create significant risk with customers.

Let's look at these challenges in greater detail.

Process Innovation

RBS understood that changes in customer solutions should drive changes in processes. For example, the mortgage advisor reviewing the accuracy of information in a digital application had to work very differently than the advisor reviewing a paper application. The bank thus needed to redesign the processes followed by its mortgage advisors when it introduced its digital mortgage application.

So how should agile teams go about innovating processes? In some ways, process innovation is much like any other agile innovation. You start with the customer and work backward to solve their needs in an incremental, iterative way. You accomplish this with empowered multidisciplinary teams. In other ways, however, the approach requires a higher level of sophistication. Companies have found two methods particularly useful.

Design Operations as Modular Capabilities

Today's software systems are typically built as microservices—small, modular units of functionality with clearly defined interfaces. Any system developer can make use of a microservice just by knowing the function it performs and understanding its interfaces. Operations capabilities can be designed in the same way. A corporate real estate function, for instance, could be given parameters for the number of people it must accommodate, the type of work these people do, and location requirements; it could then be given the task of identifying and contracting for space that would fill those specifications. A modular arrangement like this allows an agile team to improve the functioning of the capability without worrying about interfering with other parts of the organization.

Encourage Open-Market Competition for Capabilities

Just as external customers have a choice of which companies to buy from, an internal capability can determine whether it is truly world-class by giving other parts of the organization the option to use external providers. That requires capabilities designed to interface with one another in modular fashion. In the real estate example, an external supplier could also provide the service described, and the company could compare the results. Some companies go further and encourage internal capabilities to market themselves externally. Amazon Web Services is among the best-known examples (see chapter 8 for more on AWS). External commercial success is arguably the best indicator of a world-class capability. It can provide valuable funding and learning so that the capability can keep improving.

If you are on a process innovation team, you may find some other differences as well. Your primary customers may be internal customers who are working to please external customers. You might need to work with both groups. The RBS mortgage application team received input from both internal mortgage advisors and external customers applying for mortgages. Alternatively, you might be building a capability that will be used by multiple internal customers. That could require customizing solutions to each customer segment or making tough trade-offs. In upgrading its supply-chain systems, one industrial equipment manufacturer with fifty factories around the world needed to accommodate some process differences among these facilities even while it was pushing for a greater degree of standardization. Often, agile process innovation requires a heavy dose of technology. Finding people, especially product owners, who can master the necessary business and technology skills is challenging. You need special people and teams to succeed. In building its cadre of customer journey owners, RBS put significant effort into freeing up people with both sets of skills and into developing them in others.

Another challenge is managing the link with operations. Changing things that are geared to remain stable is difficult. It requires establishing effective ways for better ideas to flow from operations to teams responsible for process and technology innovation and, in turn, for the innovations developed by these teams to be implemented in operations. Companies can use a variety of techniques. Product owners may come from the operation targeted for innovation, thus providing both relevant hands-on knowledge and credibility with the team. Managers and representative front-line workers from the operation can attend sprint reviews as key stakeholders. Product owners can make a point of spending as much time as necessary discussing improvement ideas and prototypes with these representatives; some might be delegated to work closely with innovation teams to pilot changes. Operations people should be able to submit ideas through an automated system, with personal follow-up as needed. And everyone, innovation teams and ops teams together, should use the same business metrics, such as revenue growth, operating cost, reliability, or Net Promoter scores, to provide the right incentives. Our recommendation in chapter 6 to locate innovation teams within the organizational units they serve further enables change to be adopted by operations.

Technology Innovation

Agile has spread fastest among technology innovators, especially software engineers. What makes agile such an effective approach for software development? The problems to be solved are complex and the solutions initially unknown. Product requirements will most likely change. The work can be modularized and performed incrementally. Close collaboration with end users (and rapid feedback from them) is feasible. Testing can be automated. Success rates with traditional (waterfall) methods are low. But the value of success is high, especially with the increasing importance to customers of digital solutions.

We see many organizations with lots of agile technology teams, but we do not see many agile technology organizations. Technology departments have adopted agile software development extensively, yet most are not keeping pace with the changes required in business processes and customer solutions. Some of the reasons for this disappointing disparity will by now sound familiar: not working from the customer backward in deciding what to build; top-down, big-bang mandates leading to halfhearted, inconsistent adoption of agile practices; leaders who talk up agile but don't change their own management styles; rigid, slow, tedious planning, budgeting, and reviewing; compensation, promotion, and other people policies that undercut agile values. But there are other factors at play that are more specific to software development:

- *Architecture.* This is among the most important. While agile software development provides better results than traditional methods regardless of the architecture, monolithic systems can greatly compromise that improvement. If the architecture issues are left unaddressed, the results from agile will continue to feel lackluster.

- *Excessive specialization.* Software engineers often have highly specialized skills. We typically recommend that agile teams focus on solving customer problems and, when possible, stay together for months and years. But heterogeneous technologies mean the skills required to address the backlog of a complex experience team will vary. If engineers are too specialized, they will end up with teams that are too large or that consistently need to swap out members.

- *Departmental silos.* Traditionally, separate IT units are responsible for different tasks: software development, system maintenance, support, IT operations, and information security. In some industries, still more units are involved, such as legal or compliance. Each of these groups works in its own silo and is accountable for different objectives. They are often at odds with one another, causing progress to slow to a crawl. In an agile technology organization, all of the functions are performed by blended agile teams.

For purely digital products, where by definition there is no physical work involved and processes are fully encoded in software, the agile team can have end-to-end responsibility for the full product. These teams essentially combine innovation and operations. With no need to retrain people to adopt process changes, digital products can be innovated more rapidly. These characteristics explain why agile practices are so common among digital-native companies such as Google, Facebook, Twitter, and Spotify. But the benefits of agile software development are equally compelling for other firms. Moving from traditional methods to mature agile teams typically leads to productivity and speed-to-market improvements of threefold or more. The improvements can be traced to a litany of good things, including a reduction in waiting time for design decisions and approvals, less effort spent creating traditional business cases and waiting for funding, automation of IT-related tasks such as functional and security testing, automation of tasks once provided by other units such as provisioning the development environment, and aligned incentives through end-to-end ownership of the product life cycle. Even more important than these benefits, of course, is the fact that agile teams create the features that are most valuable to customers and to the business. They generally don't waste time creating features that customers do not value.

An example of a purely digital customer solution is RBS's Home Agent, which is a key to the bank's strategy of supporting customers in home buying and ownership, not just home financing. Home

Agent allows customers to get assistance on their phone with a wide range of home ownership activities, including setting a budget and shopping for a new home, home financing and refinancing, planning and funding home improvements, and tracking home equity. Employing agile teams that incorporated all the needed skills related to customer insights, software development, and third-party partnering, RBS was able to develop and launch the first version of Home Agent in four months. A customer solution of this complexity and quality would have taken at least three times as long under the previous methods—if indeed it could have been successfully developed at all.

Software development is challenging, and achieving the benefits of agile requires traditional organizations like RBS to make a wide range of changes that go beyond the principles and practices we have described for other uses. A full treatment of the requirements for effective agile software development is beyond the scope of this book, but some of them have been mentioned earlier or are listed here. Readers can find others—and a fuller explanation of all—at the website bain.com/doing-agile-right, including:

- Modular architecture, which allows each agile team to minimize interdependencies with other teams when writing code.

- Improved engineering practices and upgraded technical talent, typically requiring extensive technical training and coaching of both front-line employees and leadership, along with selective hiring to augment (and sometimes replace) current talent.

- Converged backlogs, with each agile team responsible for the development, maintenance, and support of the software that relates to its product. This end-to-end accountability creates greater ownership and is more efficient than dividing these three activities among two or three different groups.

- DevSecOps, the tools and practices that allow agile software development teams to do most of the work to move software from development to production quickly and securely.

- New IT services vendor models, often involving a shift from fixed deliverables to fixed capacity (in agile teams) as well as commitments to low turnover among team members.

- Revised location strategy enabling greater colocation and upgraded talent.

- Transformed support and control functions that succeed in their functional missions while allowing agile development teams to work at pace. One key here is to shift these functional groups' orientations from correcting work product after the fact, as is often done now, to coaching agile development teams to create compliant product from the start.

Software development is especially well suited to a key requirement of implementing agile at scale: breaking large tasks down into modular components and then reintegrating the workstreams seamlessly. Amazon can deploy software thousands of times a day in part because its IT architecture was designed to help developers make fast, frequent releases without jeopardizing the firm's complex systems. By contrast, many large companies are limited by inflexible architecture: no matter how fast they can code programs, they can deploy software only a few times a week or a month.

Achieving a modular architecture like Amazon's can seem like an insurmountable hurdle to many large companies that depend on monolithic legacy systems. It can be done, however, by applying the same customer-focused agile principles we have been discussing throughout this book. Modernizing through small steps, sequencing those steps based on the benefit they provide to customers, and using the agile software development methods described in this chapter will make the journey faster, more affordable, and less risky.

Agile Wars

One more note on technology: there are dozens of agile methods, each with its passionate advocates. The problem is that as tribes within the same company practice different agile religions for extended periods, it gets harder to bring them together. They develop habitual behaviors. They malign competitive frameworks and exaggerate the benefits of their own. This process not only causes confusion, it actually creates animosity among colleagues who should be building balanced, harmonized business systems. Nowhere do these debates grow more heated than among proponents of agile, lean, and product management methods. We have seen fierce arguments nearly erupt into fisticuffs. We do realize that the people who try to break up fights always seem to get punched in the process, but someone needs to bring some sanity to this chaos. So here we go.

Lean is a source of considerable confusion because people apply the term to two very different approaches: lean production systems (also known as Lean Six Sigma), and lean product development (also known as lean start-up).

Lean production systems are tools for running the business, for improving the quality and efficiency of operations. They increase conformance to specifications, minimizing variability and reducing waste. Lean Six Sigma demands that no more than 3.4 out of one million outputs can fail to conform. It improves efficiency by continuously reducing eight sources of waste (defects, overproduction, waiting, nonutilized talent, transportation, inventory, motion, and extra-processing).[4] We highly recommend lean production methods for improving operations. We do not recommend them for managing innovation. Innovation needs variability—even some inefficiency—to test, learn, and evolve. Some lean zealots continue to prescribe Six Sigma for innovation, but research shows that the better a culture gets at eliminating variability, the worse it gets at innovation.[5]

Lean start-up and product management are both methods for agile innovation. Lean start-up is famous for its widespread and highly publicized adoption by GE.[6] It combines lean principles with design thinking and agile approaches to foster continuous innovation the way successful start-ups do.[7] Product management encourages technology developers to think of themselves as product or brand managers who are responsible for developing profitable products that solve important customer frustrations, not just managing projects to deliver predetermined features. If the latter sounds a lot like other agile approaches, that's because it is quite similar. Two substantive differences, however, are worth noting. First, while agile uses the same approach across all innovation activities, product management concentrates on products that are powered by technology. Second, product management advocates argue (convincingly) that the product owners of too many agile teams are simply managing backlogs and are not acting like true CEOs. They are not taking full responsibility for the results of the products they develop. They are not understanding the full market context, true customer needs, competitor positions, or the financial implications of complicated trade-offs. They are not deploying persistent teams to design and scale profitable solutions.[8]

These distinctions may seem fairly minor and indeed could be helpful to agile. But they can generate a surprising amount of confusion, conflict, and inefficiency. Some advocates contend that all product management teams must be persistent and that a company should never launch temporary teams to attack urgent, short-term problems. Some organizations are adding a new layer of strategic product managers to oversee agile product owners, rather than clarifying and upgrading the product owners' jobs. Fanatics sometimes argue that product management teams are only for technology-related initiatives, forcing separate job titles, vocabularies, and training programs for technology innovations versus others. In our experience, harmonizing agile and product management methods to develop unified approaches that can be customized to the company culture and shared across the entire enterprise yields far better results than fostering adversarial dissension.

Good processes and technology are at the core of creating cost-effective solutions that customers will value. Moreover, the technologies available to automate and improve processes, such as robotic process automation and machine learning, have been growing at an accelerated pace. But the adoption of these technologies at many companies has been slow. The techniques described in this chapter should help companies to break through these barriers.

FIVE KEY TAKEAWAYS

1. Agile is for innovation, but innovation is more than creating new products and services for customers. Agile methods work equally well for improving the business processes that produce those products and services, and for improving the technology that enables those business processes.

2. Because reliability and efficiency are so important to business processes and technology, bureaucracy does everything possible to minimize variability and change. Agile approaches also encourage strict adherence to standard operating procedures, but regularly innovate to improve those procedures. They then ensure that the new procedures are accepted, incorporated in training, and properly executed.

3. Persistent, cross-functional agile teams are the best ways to improve business processes and technology. As teams gain experience and trust with operators, their development capabilities increase and adoption rates accelerate.

4. Agile teams working on business processes and technology are as customer-obsessed as those developing customer-facing products and services. Sometimes their innovations directly enhance consumer experiences. Other times, their customers are internal customers whose performance is vital to improving consumer experiences.

5. Many companies have a large number of agile technology teams, but few companies have agile technology organizations. The reasons include many of the same deviations from best practices that can inhibit any agile team plus several that are specific to software. Overcoming them involves making architecture more modular, helping engineers to become more versatile, and breaking down functional silos within and outside of IT departments.

8

DOING AGILE RIGHT

When we set out to write this book, we asked each other what we hoped readers would do differently after reading it. What was the customer problem we were trying to solve? After all, there are countless books, articles, and blogs on agile in the public domain. Why would the world need another one?

The answer was easy. We really do want agile to become a valuable and practical tool rather than one more frustrating fad. We believe that agile mindsets and methods can make people in an organization far happier and more successful. We want readers to look back on their agile transitions in five to ten years with a sense of pride and fulfillment rather than embarrassment and disappointment. Our concern is that the faddish misuse of agile will tarnish the whole idea. If fanatics try to correct one kind of imbalance by swinging all the way to its opposite—or if authoritarians use it as one more club to bludgeon people into obeying orders even faster than before—agile will soon join quality circles and business process reengineering on the aforementioned scrap heap of management manias.

And a scrap heap there is. Over the last twenty-seven years, our firm has collected candid feedback from nearly fifteen thousand executives in more than seventy countries to understand the truth about management tools of all sorts. This is probably the world's largest and longest running database on the subject, and it has allowed us to trace the popularity and effectiveness of scores of such tools over time. We have watched tools such as knowledge management, quality circles, business process reengineering, and Lean Six Sigma become popular quite suddenly, then fall out of fashion. This happens most often when tools are overhyped and misapplied to problems they were never designed to solve. Usage grows faster than satisfaction, as in that old cigarette commercial that asked whether you were "smoking more now and enjoying it less." Eventually, managers realize that the fad is no cure-all, that it has actually caused them to neglect other aspects of the business, and that analysts are now beginning to ridicule those who naïvely succumbed to the fad. At that point, usage falls fast.

Bain's obsession with the truth about tools has proved especially helpful with agile. The studies listed in appendix C support the idea that agile is no fad. So does our own experience with clients. We and our colleagues founded the Agile Enterprise Exchange to help senior executives share candid insights about their own experiences. Operating under the Chatham House Rule, a group of more than forty senior executives from a wide range of industries, geographies, and business functions agreed to meet regularly, network continuously with each other, and openly share insights into their successes and challenges.[1] This exchange is helping agile to become a valuable and sustainable trend. Much of their collective wisdom has shaped this chapter, and we are grateful to the members who are generously helping each other and others to do agile right.

Some of the guidelines for avoiding faddishness—for doing agile right—are simple and obvious, and we have mentioned them repeatedly in the book. It shouldn't generate fear, for example. Contrary to popular opinion, people don't fear all change. Most of us love vacations, better beauty products, new movies, and so on. What we fear is loss. As the psychologist Daniel Kahneman has shown, fear of loss has twice the psychological power of hope for gain. An agile transition should not provoke fear of losing control over operations, or of losing functional expertise, or of giving up current ways of working before learning that new ways are better. You can avoid fear through genuine collaboration and by iteratively prototyping, testing, and adapting proposed changes under real-life operating conditions.

Remember, too, that agile is a tool, not a strategy. A chainsaw is a wonderful tool for removing trees from fallen power lines or harvesting lumber to build a house. But no company needs a chainsaw strategy or a chief chainsaw officer. And a chainsaw is not the best tool for slicing tomatoes or performing heart surgery. Doing agile right means using agile as a tool in service of a strategy to improve business performance. It also means using the tool only where it's appropriate. Michael Porter has rightly said that the essence of strategy is choosing what not to do. We likewise believe that doing agile right means choosing where not to use it. Agile methods are designed to develop innovative solutions where what to deliver and how to deliver it are vague and unpredictable. It isn't the best way to manage routine operations, which require strict adherence to standardized operating procedures.

We also want to repeat once more that agile isn't for abrupt cost cuts. Innovative business processes eventually enable people to do more work with fewer resources. But agile is not a great method for rapidly removing 30 percent of employees. It is sometimes sold that way, because faddists have learned that bureaucrats take to cost reduction tools as felines take to catnip—especially if the tools promise to deliver growth and conceal previous management mistakes. But we hope we never hear statements like this: "We are transforming from a gravel company to a technology company, and now that we're accelerating growth by adopting agile methods, we have no choice but to lay off 30 percent of our amazing people."

Observing simple guidelines like these lets you start the journey productively. But doing it right requires more than just avoiding the obvious potholes. An agile journey really is like a triathlon: it can be a lengthy and sometimes arduous trip. So in the rest of this chapter we want to do two things. One is to recount the experience of a company—Amazon—that has created and sustained its own remarkably successful version of agile over a period of years. It's an inspiring story not because Amazon is an ideal company that should be copied—you already know what we think about copying—but because Amazon has continued to be extraordinarily innovative over a long stretch of time in a wide variety of businesses, and it's worth learning how they do it. The other task for this chapter is to distill from our own research and experience a handful of rules for the agile road. These rules won't just help you avoid the potholes; they will actually help you reach your destination.

Agile at Amazon

If the purpose of scaling agile is to create and sustain superior results by running the business reliably and efficiently, adapting the business to capitalize on unpredictable opportunities, and harmonizing the system across all these activities, then it's hard to write a book on the subject without examining Amazon's journey. Amazon's system developed over time. The company more or less invented it on its own, though CEO Jeff Bezos is famous for adopting good ideas from anyone. The system is messy and wouldn't look perfect to a purist. But it works—and it is instructive. It is also a powerful argument against those who would consider agile a fad.

As everyone knows, Amazon is a business phenomenon. An investment of $1,000 shortly after its IPO was worth $1.35 million by mid-2019. Magazines have lauded the company as most innovative, most admired, and so on. It often leads the American Customer Satisfaction Index for internet retail. It is an innovative marvel that has integrated forward and backward while adding new channels, new geographies, new categories, and new businesses. All this, of course, makes executives skeptical of its worth as an exemplar. "Who doesn't know about Amazon?" our clients sometimes tell us. "They were born agile. There's a news story every day about how they focus on the long term, take big risks, and kill or buy their competitors. I'm sick of hearing about Amazon. We have to operate in the real world. We have to make money and pay taxes. We can't hire the people they hire. We don't have their technology, and we certainly don't have their CEO."

But we're not suggesting that anyone should cut and paste the Amazon strategy. Nor are we suggesting that other companies try to transplant individual components from the Amazon system into their own. And we're certainly not suggesting that Amazon is some sort of perfect company, to be emulated in all respects. Indeed, that's what makes it such an insightful example.

Look at all the negatives. Amazon's culture does not provide the psychological safety that Google and other agile proponents recommend. Amazonians describe their culture to us as "confrontational," "intellectually intimidating," "combative," "bruising," and "Darwinian." The stack ranking and firing of good people at the wrong end of a forced bell curve is emotionally draining. People work very hard at Amazon. Finding a sustainable work/life balance can be difficult. Amazon does not talk about a grand social purpose, which many experts believe is crucial to motivation; indeed, it has been roundly criticized for its treatment of low-wage workers and its heavy-handed approach to local governments over issues of taxation and location incentives. Even internally, funding off-cycle ideas is harder than it should be in an agile enterprise. CEO Jeff Bezos and other senior executives can be notoriously demanding micromanagers. Product release dates and required features are more firm than agile practitioners typically recommend. Insiders tell us that working on failed initiatives is not nearly as fun as Bezos would lead outsiders to believe.

Any one of these weaknesses might, theoretically, impede agile operations. Collectively, they could be crippling. Yet Amazon's agile system powers ahead. How does that happen? The people we have talked to—and we're fortunate to have many close relationships with executives who have worked at all levels of Amazon over the years—describe a balanced system of strengths and weaknesses that have evolved over time to work together in a uniquely Amazon way. It's about the system, not the individuals. Thousands of Amazonians rotate in and out of the company all the time, so other companies can and do hire them. Amazon people are neither demigods nor demons. They are real people who accomplish extraordinary results in the Amazon system.

Jason Goldberger is one such person. Goldberger arrived at Amazon as a senior buyer in 1999, six years out of college and two years after the company's initial public offering. Over the next eight years, he would advance to divisional merchandise manager, senior category manager, and eventually to general manager. He would battle through the dot-com crash from 2000 through 2002, when Amazon's stock price plummeted by 95 percent. He would also participate in the evolution of Amazon's unique agile system. That system helped the company rebound during his time there, pushing revenues from $2 billion to $15 billion, employees from 7,600 to 17,000, and the stock price from its 2001 low to a 1,300 percent increase.

Like other observers and participants, Goldberger found the most striking characteristic of Amazon's system to be its obsession over customers. He had worked at other retailers—Federated Department Stores, QVC, and Linens 'n Things—so he understood what terms like *customer centricity* were supposed to mean. But it was different at Amazon. The company was crazy, nuts, loony about customers. Executives would routinely wake up software engineers in the middle of the night to solve customer problems. They would readily sacrifice short-term profits for the long-term goal of delighting customers. Amazon tracks some five hundred metrics, and nearly 80 percent of them relate to customers. Bezos frequently leaves one seat empty at a conference table for "the most important person in the room."[2]

Every Amazon executive we know agrees with Goldberger that Amazon takes its mission to be "Earth's most customer-centric company" far more seriously than other companies may imagine. It enforces a strong set of operating principles to reinforce this obsession.[3] The principles include ownership (think long term on behalf of the entire company); invent and simplify (look everywhere for new ideas); be right a lot (build strong judgment from diverse perspectives); learn and be curious (constantly improve); hire and develop the best (raise the performance bar with every hire and promotion); insist on the highest standards (even if others think they are unreasonably high); think big (communicate a bold direction); have a bias for action (speed matters); be frugal (accomplish more with less); earn trust (be vocally self-critical); dive deep (stay connected to details); have backbone (respectfully challenge and avoid compromise); and deliver results (never settle).[4] Most companies have platitudinous principles, and most employees learn quickly that those principles don't mean a thing. The executives we talk to say that Amazon is different. The principles are the criteria Amazon uses to hire builders and the principles by which it lets them build. They are how the company runs its business. Love them or hate them, you will live or die by these principles at Amazon.

Genuine customer obsession sets a strong foundation for agility. Still, caring without creating strong capabilities won't build an agile enterprise.

Goldberger, for example, was a merchant. But he learned quickly that he couldn't really take care of customers the way Amazon expected him to unless he learned a lot more about technology and supply chains. So he worked side by side with operations experts. He researched discussion topics that he didn't fully grasp. He came to understand and appreciate functions that seemed foreign in previous jobs. He describes this learning process as being common among Amazonians.

Starting around 2000, when Amazon had nine thousand people, Goldberger noticed that the company began thinking of its technological capabilities in new ways. It started to break large, monolithic systems into smaller service modules called microservices. Each microservice would be built as an independent, flexible, reusable, and replaceable subsystem that would communicate with other microservices through standard connections known as application programming interfaces. This approach improved efficiency. Building small modules made it faster and easier for autonomous teams to develop, test, deploy, and scale their services. Equally important, it improved Amazon's ability to quickly identify, stop, and replace any microservice that was not working properly. Microservices were a counterbalance to the sharp elbows that could have made widespread collaboration difficult. They made cross-organizational collaboration and experimentation far less risky.

These service-oriented architectures were, and are, a key component of Amazon's agile system. "Most people think that the most valuable contribution of service-oriented architectures is the ability to release innovations faster," Goldberger told us.

> Yes, it does that. But it also lets you stop ineffective innovations faster. If you tell people to innovate without making mistakes, you will kill innovation. But if you tell people to innovate and not worry about mistakes that are quickly reversible, you free them to test and learn in more agile ways. Jeff talks about two-way doors, where you can always come back if you don't like what you see on the other side. Service-oriented architectures enabled thousands of two-way doors.

One of the earliest applications of this architectural philosophy was Amazon Marketplace, a platform that let Amazon sell third-party inventories on its website. Amazon had tried twice before—

with Amazon Auctions and zShops—to offer competitive alternatives to eBay. Both flopped. But service-oriented architectures enabled Amazon to create single detail pages that seamlessly integrated third-party providers into the core Amazon shopping experience. Now the company had turned a me-too idea into a superior offering. Today, there are more than five million marketplace sellers on Amazon's platform, accounting for 53 percent of its retail units sold.

The philosophy also led to the creation of Amazon Web Services. In 2003, two members of Amazon's website engineering team, Benjamin Black and Chris Pinkham, began working on ways to scale the company's technology infrastructure faster and more efficiently to keep up with the company's skyrocketing growth. They wrote a memo describing the cloud-based architecture and analyzing the potential to sell virtual servers as a service. Although Amazon's board feared the idea was too far from the company's core retail concept, Bezos liked the way it could help anyone, including students in dorm rooms, to start new businesses. Amazon officially relaunched Amazon Web Services in 2006. Since then, it has created a new strategic engine for Amazon, providing strong revenue and profit growth for the company and contributing key breakthroughs in cloud computing for the world.

Despite the entrepreneurial values and principles that permeated all of Amazon, its organizational structure for a long time remained very much like that of most companies. In early 2002, Bezos decided to change that. He formally proposed scaling agile teams, though he called them two-pizza teams and was largely indifferent to the specific methods or frameworks they used. His idea was to restructure the whole enterprise around small, autonomous teams that would continuously tackle the biggest problems in more agile ways. Each team needed to have no more than ten people—small enough to feed with two pizzas when members were working late into the night. The teams were free to compete with each other. Each one would create a fitness function, an equation that would help themselves and others (especially Bezos) to measure their progress.

Goldberger recalls how eager people were to work on these pizza teams. "Pizza teams are brilliant. They strip away unnecessary hierarchy and let people who are closest to the work collaborate directly with each other and with customers. Most people I knew wanted to try them. Those that did try them got a pizza icon by their name in the online directory, which was a badge of honor."

Two-pizza teams took off and stuck in innovative departments such as technology, but not in routine operations such as accounting. The fitness functions never gained much traction anywhere and were mostly ignored. Amazon did not end up restructuring the whole enterprise around two-pizza teams, but the teams have become the primary mechanisms for attacking innovative ideas. Amazon runs thousands of them, and they have become a core part of the culture.

In 2004, a decade after the company's founding, Amazon also changed its approach to funding innovative initiatives and running proposal discussions. Today, every plan and every proposal—especially those for two-pizza teams—begins with a six-page memo. The memo opens with a visionary one- or two-page press release of the benefits the initiative would create for customers. Very much like the user stories in any agile backlog, mock press releases describe targeted customers, the benefits they are seeking, the frustrations they have experienced with previous solutions, and the advantages of the new Amazon approach. The proposal also includes at least four or five pages of frequently asked questions (FAQs)—starting first with the hardest ones—about how the innovation works. Frequently the memo includes exhibits and rough diagrams or pictures depicting customers using the solutions. Although these proposals were originally dubbed six-page memos, many executives now refer to them as "PR/FAQs," and many memos run fifteen pages or more.

Goldberger still remembers his first six-page proposal. He had prepared a PowerPoint presentation but learned one week before that it needed to be a six-page memo. "It was a rough and tumble discussion," he says. "It's a little awkward to sit there for thirty to sixty minutes while everyone reads the memo. Then the questions start flying in random order. If you don't know your stuff, you will be exposed within minutes. Bezos can trip up a canned answer in a heartbeat. You had to be an expert, not just a competent presenter." What Goldberger appreciated most about the six-page memos, however, was how they reinforced Amazon's mission about customer focus. "What I remember," he told us "is how they made me feel. They made us all think about what we were really trying to do. Working backward from the customer forces you to think about every activity as a service to the customer. And since many of the proposals are focused on improving internal business processes and technology, it makes you think about everyone you work with as a customer. I felt like I had a real responsibility to them, and I developed deep commitments to them."

Other executives agree with Goldberger, including Nadia Shouraboura, an executive at Amazon from 2004 through 2012. "Each piece of Amazon's system balances and reinforces other parts of the system," she told us.

> The core of the system is obsession over customers. Amazon might micromanage, but it's usually about customer passion. Personally, I prefer this passion to indifference. Executives don't tell people what to do. They say, "You are responsible for this customer, and this customer has this problem. What are you going to do about it?" Six-page memos secure resources for innovation by working from the customer backward. During my time at Amazon, I wrote hundreds of six-page memos and read thousands more. Those discussions do not waste time on what presenters want to say. They spend every possible minute on reinventing customer experiences. Then two-pizza teams focus on how to develop creative solutions for the customers. Two-pizza teams are self-sufficient, fully committed and empowered. Each team is what Amazon calls "single-threaded," meaning they do not multitask. One team, one problem. Service-oriented

architectures enable those teams to collect customer data from anywhere, and test solutions anywhere, without waiting for approvals from hierarchies. The system works to make everyone better.

Amazon continues to expand and refine its tools for scaling and improving agility. Will it succeed in the future? Bezos doesn't know, and neither do we. In November 2018, he told his employees, "Amazon is not too big to fail. . . . In fact, I predict one day Amazon will fail. Amazon will go bankrupt. If you look at large companies, their lifespans tend to be thirty-plus years, not a hundred-plus years." The key to postponing that demise is for the company to obsess over customers and to avoid looking inward. "If we start to focus on ourselves, instead of focusing on our customers, that will be the beginning of the end. We have to try and delay that day for as long as possible."[5]

The dangers of a complex system are real, even for Amazon. Regulatory changes could force breakups. Growth could slow, which would affect the stock price and the compensation of star players. Micromanagement and bureaucracy could increase, smothering innovation. Recent declines in customer satisfaction could turn into long-term trends. But we know of few companies working harder to continuously balance and harmonize its system to adapt to unpredictable markets than Amazon.

The Rules of the Agile Road

Most of the companies that succeed at agile, including Amazon and the others named in this book, seem to develop an unusual set of capabilities. These capabilities enable them to implement agile without falling into the traps and faddishness that plague so many other would-be agilists. Four are particularly important—so important that we think of them as the rules of the agile road, the skills and attributes that will take you where you want to go.

1. Learn to Love Agile Teams—and Then Create Your Own

You can't consider doing agile at scale if you can't do agile at all. As we have noted, agile teams are tools used to develop innovative solutions when what to deliver, how to deliver it, or both are vague and unpredictable. Their primary purpose is to change the business through innovation—developing new products, services, or customer experiences (for external customers); improving processes to help operations folks deliver solutions to those external customers; or improving the technology that underlies those processes. Teams are at the heart of agile.

People sponsoring or participating in agile teams should not only be familiar with agile practices; they should also understand *why* the teams do everything they do. The teams are self-governing because autonomy increases motivation, puts decisions in the hands of people closest to customers and operations, and gives leaders time to focus on enterprise strategies that only they can do. The teams are small and multidisciplinary because small size improves communications and productivity, and because including a variety of disciplines increases creativity, reduces interdependencies with other teams, and accelerates decision making. Teams are dedicated to a single task because multitasking makes people stupid, slows development cycles, and increases work in process. Effective agile teams do not blindly follow rules. They understand why they are doing what they are doing, continually search for better ways to do it, and share their insights with other teams.

Wherever they are deployed, agile teams should create irrefutable results. Great results build enthusiasm for expanding the scale and scope of agile. Great results attract star players. As more people join teams, they gain confidence. They learn the value of prioritization. They begin challenging the assumptions behind predictions. They collect direct feedback from customers rather than from managers, limit work in process, and speed up decision making. They figure out how to eliminate low-value work and how to continuously improve their own ways of working. They then carry this confidence

back to their functional departments. The agile teams learn to identify impediments to their speed and success, and the leadership team
learns how to remove these impediments. Agile teams are pulled,
not pushed, into the organization.

As you learn to love agile teams, you will want to create your
own team, one that is committed to working together according to
agile principles. If you are a C-level executive, this may be your executive leadership team or the senior managers of the business unit
or function you lead. If you are a junior executive, it may be a group
of people in your department. Maybe it is a team currently working on innovation projects in more traditional ways. Or perhaps it
is a group of people who do similar work, but have never considered doing it together as an agile team.

Start by getting your team to read and discuss this book together.
Debate the concepts. Work with team members to study and experiment with various aspects of agile methods. Find out whether there
are effective agile teams somewhere in the company that you can
visit and observe. Ask them frank questions about what they like
and dislike about agile approaches. Ask your team if they would like
to pursue an opportunity or two in agile fashion. Consider joining
a training program together to build a common foundation of capabilities. Work together to build sustainable agile habits. Write your
own personal version of an agile manifesto.

When one of us (Darrell) was first learning agile principles and
practices, he figured he should practice them himself. For each value
in the agile manifesto, he picked one simple behavior to change and
set promptings to trigger that behavior. For example:

- *Work in ways that make humans happy and successful.* When
  he felt stressed, he determined to express sincere appreciation
  for the work of at least one person.

- *Break large tasks into small steps and test solutions with
  working models.* When confronted by an opinion different
  from his own, he decided to ask, "How could we test that?"

- *Simplify and sequence activities to focus on the most valuable customer benefits.* When asked to do work with little or no value to customers, he committed to describe what he needed to do instead and to explain the extraordinary value that would be forfeited by delays.

- *Welcome and celebrate learning.* When his predictions or opinions turned out to be wrong, he vowed to laugh about them with others and change course.

What happened? Here's his account:

> I found that the most enjoyable change was the first. Expressing gratitude made me happier and improved teamwork. The hardest change was the last. For more than a year, I wrote down my hypotheses and predictions, then tracked their accuracy using something called a Brier score. Embarrassingly, I found that I was wrong far more often than I expected. Along with a heavy dose of humility came the realization that considering the opinions of others couldn't be much riskier than relying on my own. I also feared that laughing at so many mistakes would undermine my credibility. Instead, it led to more collaborative ways of developing hypotheses, better results, and greater confidence.

As these behaviors became easier, he started adding others. He felt happier and more in control. He set a better example for his teams and developed lifelong habits that would never slip back to bureaucratic behaviors.

2. Master Agile at Scale—but Envision an Agile Enterprise

Agile at scale, remember, refers to widespread proliferation of agile teams, even when agile principles have not spread to the rest of the enterprise. Its most obvious benefit is that it expands the quality and quantity of innovation. It infuses a spirit of testing and learning into the business, encouraging employees to identify opportunities for improvement in everything they do. Moreover, it can increase innovation without increasing costs. Leaders who inventory current innovation activities often find themselves astonished by how many projects there are, where those projects are, what they are doing or not doing, who is working on them (and what else those people are working on), how effectively they are coordinating, and how well they are turning out innovations. The executives typically find that a third of these teams could cease operations tomorrow and never be missed. Stopping those projects outright creates room and resources for more valuable opportunities. Among the other two-thirds, some teams will be working on vital initiatives but will be struggling and discouraged. These are good candidates for agile makeovers. Sometimes leaders must reconfigure the teams to add the right skills and mindsets, but the subsequent improvements in costs and results can create striking success stories and enthusiastic ambassadors.

Another benefit of scaling agile may be even more important. The proliferation of teams teaches people how teams of teams can work within familiar bureaucratic structures, such as matrix organizations and hierarchies. Cross-functional agile teams are by definition matrix organizations. As long as the people to whom team members report understand agile mindsets and methods, the joint accountability doesn't hamper performance. The same is true for hierarchies. Teams of agile teams, and teams of teams of agile teams, create reporting structures that look a lot like hierarchies. Yet product owners are not traditional bosses: they do not predict, command, or control the work of teams. Nor do they assign tasks to individuals or set deadlines—the team works together to do these things. Despite all the criticisms of hierarchies, they, too, work well with agile mindsets and methods. Mastering agile at scale not only improves innovation, it also helps operations to run in ways that are more humane.

Mastering agile at scale requires that leaders know enough to define what they mean by *agile*. As we noted in chapter 2, there are dozens of agile frameworks. When most of our clients examine the options, they typically choose two or three frameworks (for example, Scrum, Kanban, and a scaling framework such as Scrum@Scale or SAFe). They then customize these frameworks to fit their company's culture, harmonize the core concepts and terminologies, and encourage teams to adapt.

Though agile at scale is a great start, doing agile right ultimately requires both agile teams and agile systems—an agile enterprise. We know that these terms are frequently confused because both involve doing agile. But the differences are important. Agile at scale focuses on improving the performance of agile teams, allowing bureaucracy and innovation to coexist. Agile enterprises focus on creating agile business systems, transforming bureaucracy and innovation into symbiotic partners that collaborate to deliver superior results.

Let's put the concept of an agile enterprise concept under a microscope. A detailed definition might look something like this: *Agile enterprises create balanced systems that efficiently adapt to changing customer opportunities in order to deliver superior results.* Each element is meaningful, starting with the thing itself. In an agile enterprise, executives do not focus on optimizing the performance of individual teams. They focus instead on improving the performance of the entire business system. Such a system is *balanced*: it runs operations reliably and efficiently while also innovating to capitalize on changes. Stable operations and flexible innovation are not enemies. They are complementary, interdependent, mutually beneficial capabilities that need each other to survive.

The other elements are equally significant. Agile systems *efficiently adapt*. The trick in successful evolution is to preserve the characteristics that work well while quickly and efficiently changing what needs to change. Iterative testing with rapid feedback loops is the only way to adapt without creating painful, unintended consequences. And what do the systems adapt to? *Changing customer opportunities.* Agile enterprises don't merely study the customer environment to identify and react to changes in customer preferences.

As at Amazon, they proactively change the environment. They obsess over discovering, creating, and capitalizing on solutions that help customers to achieve satisfying goals and force competitors to follow their lead or face extinction. This process can and often should include disruptive innovations—products or services that a company's existing customers may not immediately value but that others might.

Finally, agile enterprises *deliver superior results*. The only valid purpose for increasing agility is to improve results—customer results (buying behaviors, market share), financial results (revenue growth, cash flows), employee results (employee quality, effectiveness), and societal results (human rights, environmental sustainability). There is nothing inherently virtuous in agility or, for that matter, nothing inherently evil in bureaucracy. They are only tools in the service of a strategy for achieving results.

Even if you are not currently planning a transition to an agile enterprise, we recommend taking a few weeks to explore what such a transition might look like. How many teams could we have? What would they do and where would they report? How much additional value could the enterprise create? How could we better harmonize bureaucracy with innovation? What would be the greatest impediments and risks to achieving such a vision? How far could we realistically go, and how fast could we plan to get there? Envisioning an agile system in this manner encourages holistic, integrative thinking. It creates an estimate of the value at stake, and it fosters greater alignment on the ultimate destination, which helps to guide strategic decisions.

There are other benefits as well. Envisioning an agile enterprise can increase commitment, energy, and the courage to take actions. It can prevent the organization from doing things that would ultimately make enterprise agility harder or impossible. It can facilitate discussions on how far toward an agile enterprise the organization wants to go, how fast it wants to get there, and how to sequence action steps. It can help the executive team identify questions that need to be answered, risks that need to be addressed, and tests that could alter decisions.

For all that, it can also lead to dangerous extremes. One extreme is, "I want it all, and I want it now." The other is, "I'm paralyzed by the prospects."

We have discussed the dangers of big-bang, all-at-once agile transitions. Executives who want it all right now typically use bureaucratic transformation teams to force agile on the organization. They almost always copy someone else's agile model, convince themselves that it has all the answers, and go for it. The results are seldom good. In a complex system like a business, the relationships among causes and effects are often delayed, and may lead to unintended consequences. Remember Prohibition: How many people expected that the amendment banning alcohol sales in the United States would also increase the wealth and power of organized crime, lead to rising use of hard drugs and dangerous homemade brews, decrease tax revenues, criminalize millions of previously law-abiding citizens, reduce trust in authority, and overburden the legal system? And still it took thirteen years for the United States to reverse course.

At the other extreme lie executives who are paralyzed by the complexity of an agile enterprise. Yes, the pain of overextended bureaucracy is harsh, and the vision of an agile enterprise is enticing. But where to begin? There is so much to change. If we don't do it perfectly, we could end up in a worse position than we are today. Fear of loss kicks in. Nothing significant happens for years. Then, suddenly, the management team realizes that they are in deep trouble. Now there is no time for delay or testing and learning. "We need it all, and we need it now." Like yo-yo dieters, such companies are apt to lurch back and forth from one extreme to another.

3. Use Agile Innovation to Get There

At the beginning of an agile journey, the hardest truth for many executives to accept is that where to go and how to get there are not just unknown, they are unknowable. Even experienced agile practitioners can't predict with any degree of confidence how agile the business system should ultimately be or how to get from here to there. This distressing prospect challenges many leaders' most fundamental assumption about how they add value. Who could argue against the philosophy of ("Neutron") Jack Welch? "Good business leaders create a vision, articulate the vision, passionately own the vision, and relentlessly drive it to completion."[6] In other words, leaders predict, command, and control.

The problem is that predicting, commanding, and controlling don't work in vague and uncertain conditions. In Amar Bhidé's study of entrepreneurial companies, he found that two-thirds of the companies moderately or significantly altered their initial visions for the enterprise before they achieved success. In his words, "Entrepreneurs revise their hypotheses rapidly through a series of experiments and adaptive responses to unforeseen problems and opportunities."[7] Famed venture capitalist Fred Wilson, cofounder of Union Square Ventures, discovered a similar pattern. "Of the twenty-six companies that I consider realized or effectively realized in my personal track record, seventeen of them made complete transformations or partial transformations of their businesses between the time we invested and the time we sold. That means there's a two-thirds chance you'll have to significantly reinvent your business between the time you take a venture capital investment and when you exit your business." Wilson further found that of the investments he considered failures, 80 percent failed to transform.[8]

As we noted earlier, scholars such as Daniel Kahneman suggest that leaders' predictions are about as accurate as the toss of a coin.[9] So if leaders' predictions are just as likely to be wrong as right, then attempts to command and control provoke a flood of humbling questions. What if my predictions are no better than those of people closer to our customers and the operations that serve them? What if testing and learning with customers actually leads to faster and better decisions than I am making? What if the time it takes to get on my calendar and wait for me to make decisions is doubling or tripling our cycle times and lead times? And so on.

Remember: Agile was designed to create innovative solutions when what to deliver and how to deliver it are vague and unpredictable. This is a perfect description of the journey from an overextended bureaucracy to an agile enterprise. And it's why we argue that your first step should be to create an agile leadership team, which will operate just like any other agile team. It has an initiative owner who is responsible for overall results and a facilitator who coaches team members and helps keep everyone actively engaged. Leaders agree to spend less time micromanaging their individual functions. They agree to spend more time developing an agile system to support the strategy for achieving targeted outcomes, such as business purposes, financial results, customer satisfaction, and employee inspiration. They overcome organizational paralysis by breaking complex problems into actionable steps and systematically attacking them. They plunge in to solve problems and remove constraints rather than delegate that work to subordinates.

A critical tool for the team is a robust, adaptive backlog of opportunities that team members can tackle together. The backlog will give your team a realistic, itemized, fact-based vision of how much value is possible, and in what order the team should attack the work. Committing to each other to stick together in pursuit of the backlog increases the probability of the team's collective success. Initially, a backlog may seem like nothing more than a fancy to-do list, but it is different in three important ways. First, each item is written in the form of an important customer need or opportunity rather than as a task to complete. Second, each item is ruthlessly sequenced to discourage multitasking and to push all resources to the most valuable work. Third, backlogs are continuously updated and resequenced to reflect the most current information about their value and resource requirements.

In addition to forcing focus on customers and adaptability, a backlog gives your agile team courage to say no to low-value activities.

When Erik Martella, vice president of Central Coast Wineries at Constellation Wines, started implementing agile, he received an email from a superior in Constellation's corporate office suggesting that the winery explore a personal passion of the sender. Previously, Martella told us, he might have responded, "OK, we'll jump right on it." Instead, he replied that the winery was following agile principles: the idea would be added to the list of potential opportunities and prioritized. As it happened, the executive liked that approach—and when he was informed that his suggestion had been assigned a low priority, he readily accepted the decision.

There's one more related benefit of a backlog. Do you remember how Amazon's Goldberger talked about the advantages of stopping ineffective innovations faster? Members of failing teams—fearing that they will be labeled as losers and reassigned to menial tasks or even laid off—work very hard to look busy and confident. They should actually be calling it quits and seeking more promising assignments. A robust backlog encourages such behavior by constantly presenting an appealing menu of obviously superior opportunities. The backlog beckons: Would you rather plug away on that mundane project delivering disappointing results or leap to one of the company's highest and most exhilarating priorities? People don't deliberately choose to fail if they have better options.

Over time, the agile leadership team (like every other agile team) must measure its progress. A common cry in the agile community these days is, "Measure outcomes, not outputs." We understand the intent, but the truth is that to create effective systems leaders need to measure outcomes *and* outputs, as well as activities, inputs, and purposes. The agile community's point is that you can work hard and turn out a bunch of new products without improving customer satisfaction or financial results. Conversely, however, you can't improve customer satisfaction or financial results without working very hard and turning out a bunch of new products.

Sakishi Toyoda, the founder of Toyota Industries and a pioneer of agile innovation methods, taught that if you want to improve outcomes, you have to improve the processes and systems that deliver those results. If outcomes weren't what was expected, he encouraged people to dig deeply into the root cause. He called his technique the five whys. Identify a problem and then ask why the processes are leading to it. If a process is defective, ask why. Keep this up until you find the source of the problem, which usually takes five iterations. Then you can figure out how to fix it. Similarly, measuring outcomes is not sufficient. You can't fix an outcome without understanding and fixing the processes in the system that cause it. Using metrics to monitor processes not only helps to answer the five whys, it also enables statistical process controls to prevent future problems even when current outcomes appear to be fine. Current financials may look strong, but if the new product pipeline is empty and your best innovators are jumping ship, you have a process problem that will soon become an outcomes problem.

As leaders do all this, their own productivity and morale improve. They learn to speak the language of the teams they are empowering. They experience common challenges and learn how to overcome them. They recognize and stop behaviors that impede agile teams. They learn to simplify and focus work. Results improve, increasing confidence and engagement throughout the organization.

4. Make It Fun

We are perplexed by how many change-management gurus preach, and actually seem to believe, that transitioning to agile approaches must be radical and painful in order to be beneficial. They seem to revel in the organizational chaos while predicting that euphoria is surely just around the corner. With all due respect to Elisabeth Kübler-Ross and grief curves, doing agile right has little in common with losing a loved one. It has everything to do with finding better ways to work in teams that make people happier, more innovative, and more successful.

Here's our advice: If the change process is making you or your employees unhappy, stop it! Now! Don't do weird things. And don't mistake employees' gradual, grudging resignation to weird ways of working for budding enthusiasm. The truth is that agile progress should feel good from the beginning. We're not saying that agile requires no work; we are saying that it should produce the equivalent of a runner's high—the good feelings that come from a workout that delivers tangible progress toward a healthier mind and body. Substantial research shows that happiness and innovation are inextricably linked. It doesn't matter whether happiness drives innovation or innovation increases happiness. If you improve one, you will begin a cycle that can continuously improve both. Success is habit forming. Our brains produce neurochemicals that make the process of successful achievement feel good. When we set and achieve a goal, our brains release dopamine, the reward hormone that drives us to continue doing things that bring us pleasure. When we bond with others and increase our trust in them, our brains deliver a hit of oxytocin, which increases loyalty and makes us want to grow closer to others. When we overcome a difficult challenge, our brains release endorphins, creating good moods and decreasing fatigue. When we engage in activities that reinforce a strong sense of purpose, our bodies produce serotonin, which makes us feel confident and calm. All of these chemicals and others reinforce beneficial behaviors and increase our happiness as well as our ability to innovate as a team.

When people are unhappy at work, it is because they are not doing rewarding things and their brains are not producing enough of the chemicals that make work pleasurable. These people aren't just disengaged, they are suffering from a form of neurochemical withdrawal. Good agile leaders will learn how to increase achievement by making innovation fun and rewarding. They learn how to help teams set and achieve goals, bond with others, overcome difficult challenges, reinforce a sense of purpose, and make successful achievements feel good.

One tactic for making the whole endeavor fun is to create and celebrate frequent wins. Critics of agile teams complain that agile uses sprints to create high-pressure deadlines that push people to exhaustion, leaving no time for resting or even thinking. We agree that bad agile has the potential to do this. But doing agile right uses sprints for entirely different purposes. By breaking large, complex problems into more manageable tasks, agile increases confidence to tackle the most daunting assignments. To figure out creative ways to develop and test rapid prototypes, agile teams employ short, tight feedback loops that quickly and easily adjust to unpredictable events. And the greatest benefit of sprints is that they create more frequent wins and opportunities to celebrate them. Teresa Amabile and Steven J. Kramer put it this way in their HBR article, "The Power of Small Wins":

> Of all the things that can boost emotions, motivation, and perceptions during a workday, the single most important is making progress in meaningful work. And the more frequently people experience that sense of progress, the more likely they are to be creatively productive in the long run. Whether they are trying to solve a major scientific mystery or simply produce a high-quality product or service, everyday progress—even a small win—can make all the difference in how they feel and perform.[10]

Managed properly, sprints create opportunities every week or two to deliver gratifying progress toward a meaningful purpose. All learning becomes something to celebrate, even if it causes the team to change assumptions, pivot to a different solution, or jump to a new opportunity. Your job as an agile leader will be to help your team create more frequent wins and to remove the obstacles that impede progress. You have the responsibility to highlight progress, and to celebrate that progress in rousing ways. Doing so will improve your team's motivation and ability to innovate.

And finally, one more ingredient of fun: teaching and coaching others. Teaching—and watching others learn—is one of the most rewarding and satisfying of human endeavors.

Here's why: Richard Feynman, whose work in quantum electrodynamics won him a Nobel Prize in Physics, taught that the best way to master any new skill was to teach it to a beginner. He believed that experts often hide behind jargon and esoteric vocabulary to disguise their own ignorance. We ourselves find that when we work to explain things in simple language, we have identified an opportunity to learn more. We try to dig in until we can explain it to a child—or to a skeptical senior executive. As you develop agile capabilities and start teaching them to beginners, you will be surprised by how much they force you to learn. Their questions will expose your incomplete thinking and hidden assumptions. And as others learn and apply agile principles and practices, improving their own performance, and making it easier for additional employees to improve theirs, you will be astonished by the satisfaction that comes from mentoring and bonding with others while making such a meaningful contribution to business performance.

As we said at the start of this book, if you and your team are not having fun with agile, you're not doing it right.

Appendix A

A LEADERSHIP TEAM'S AGILE MANIFESTO

In 2001, seventeen self-described "organizational anarchists" met for three days to discuss more adaptive ways of developing software. They released what they called the Manifesto for Agile Software Development, describing the practices they had learned to value most:

- individuals and interactions over processes and tools
- working software over comprehensive documentation
- customer collaboration over contract negotiation
- responding to change over following a plan

As we serve clients transitioning to agile enterprises, we often facilitate similar discussions with their agile leadership teams, helping them to customize and commit to their own version of an agile manifesto. By the end of the discussion, the leadership team develops a simple statement of their agile values, and members of the team commit to changing their personal behaviors to reinforce those values. They also agree to help each other monitor behaviors and correct inappropriate actions. You can see a representative example of a manifesto in figure A-1.

Behind each bullet are specific values and practices that provide greater detail on each behavior. Over the years, we have helped to develop many manifestos. Each is unique to a specific organization, but below are some common discussion topics and commitments:

INDIVIDUALS AND INTERACTIONS OVER PROCESSES AND TOOLS

- We set out a clear ambition (*what* and *why*) and metrics for success, but delegate the *how* to the team.

    - We **build strong leadership alignment** around our company strategy and priorities—the *what*.

    - We create and communicate a **compelling, clear purpose**—the *why*.

    - We use **regular business reviews** (e.g., quarterly) to maintain our alignment and focus.

    - We establish a **few critical metrics** for success as opposed to a long list of interesting data points.

    - We track progress through **active, personal engagement** with teams and in demonstrations, rather than by detailed tracking of milestones.

- We empower our teams and believe that the right answer lies not with us but within the team.

    - **We stop talking and listen deeply** to our teams; we state our own ignorance to solutions.

An agile leadership team's manifesto

Individuals and interactions over processes and tools

We set a clear ambition (*what* and *why*) and metrics for success, but delegate the *how* to the team.

We empower teams and believe that the right answer lies not with us, but within the team.

Working solutions over excessive documentation

We engage on good enough working solutions versus demanding perfect ones.

We protect the team so that they can focus; we rapidly unblock key impediments.

We support teams in breaking down complex problems and frequently delivering working solutions.

Customer engagement over rigid contracts

We encourage teams to seek out feedback from a diverse set of customers and promote a culture of rapid adaptation to customer feedback.

We believe that things can always be improved.

Responding to change over following a plan

We celebrate learning and create a safe environment for teams to take prudent risks and test unconventional hypotheses.

We embrace ruthless and constant prioritization, and stop activities that are not yielding results within the defined time frame.

We role model agile ways of working every day

- We articulate our strategies and milestones as **problems to be solved, not solutions.**

- We **push decisions down** to the people who are closest to our customers, operations, and processes.

- We **encourage everyone to contribute** to conversations.

- We **hold the team accountable** for results.

- We **treat teams and each other as partners and ask instead of answer**—for example, "What do you recommend?" and "How could we test that?"

- We regularly **observe Scrum team ceremonies** to show we believe the answers lie with them.

- We **actively seek diverse and divergent opinions** instead of looking for others who will affirm our current ideas.

WORKING SOLUTIONS OVER EXCESSIVE DOCUMENTATION

- We engage on **good enough working solutions** instead of demanding perfect.

  - We ask our teams to share **ideas and prototypes at an early state** and give feedback that can be incorporated.

  - **We don't pick apart early prototypes** but allow customers to use prototypes to shape innovation.

- We protect the team so that the member can focus and rapidly unblock key impediments.

  - We maintain a **prioritized list of impediments** and make eliminating them our top priority.

  - We **ruthlessly cancel meetings** or compress them and instead attend team coordination meetings (daily or weekly) to see how we can help.

- We **reduce demands for reporting** on progress and instead use transparency, returning to teams to see demonstrations of working products and results, and to provide feedback.

- We **eliminate traditional steering committees** with arduous management approval processes.

• We support teams in breaking down complex problems and delivering working solutions in every sprint.

- We **help our teams crack open big problems** to find ways to solve increments.

- We **say no to slides describing solutions** and ask to see real working prototypes.

- We **attend team demonstrations** to provide feedback, and see how customers react.

CUSTOMER ENGAGEMENT OVER RIGID CONTRACTS

• We encourage teams to **seek out feedback** from a diverse set of customers and promote a **culture of rapid adaptation** to customer feedback.

- We **clearly define who our customer is,** and we listen to customers *before* building something.

- We **prohibit pitches that don't have real experimental results** from real customers.

- We encourage everyone to spend more time outside the office—**Go see 'em.**

- We **avoid customer surrogates**—go directly to customers for feedback.

- We **regularly ask for assumptions** and explanations of how they are being tested with customers.

- – We **put more weight on customer-related KPIs** than on purely internal ones.

- – We **bring customers into project teams** and meetings.

- – We **equip teams to solicit customer feedback** as opposed to having that capability live outside teams.

- – We **create movement makers** who ask customer feedback questions in all meetings.

- – We **structure meetings** so team engagement with customers gets most of the airtime.

- We believe that **things can always be improved.**

  - – We **never allow a priority product to be done,** but continuously ask: How could we make it even better?

  - – We **look forward** to what our customers will need and how our market is evolving to push innovation.

RESPONDING TO CHANGE OVER FOLLOWING A PLAN

- We celebrate learning and create a **safe environment** for teams to take **prudent risks** and **test unconventional hypotheses.**

  - – We **ask *why not*** as opposed to *why* and establish opportunities for pilots, prototypes, and experimentation.

  - – We **provide the space to experiment;** we minimize the need for multiple layers of sign-off, especially when experimenting.

  - – We **advertise successes;** we tell stories at company events and recognize people who are looking ahead and identifying opportunities.

- We **seek out the bad news;** we make people feel psychologically safe sharing failures.

- We **engage in uncomfortable conversations** with customers, clients, and associates.

- We reward people from all functions and levels for bringing **new or unconventional ideas.**

- We **reward learning from failures.**

- We as leaders **admit failure publicly.**

• We embrace **ruthless** and **constant prioritization** and **stop activities that are not yielding sufficient learning and results** within the defined time frame.

- **We ruthlessly focus on our top priorities,** and get them done before tackling the next.

- We make all prioritization, work items, and **problems visible to everyone.**

- We establish a leadership team that **continuously reprioritizes the company backlog based on internal and external** feedback.

- **We stop investment** once we see we are not generating sufficient results.

• **We role model agile ways of working every day.**

- **We reduce our time in meetings** by half to allow for time to spend with customers and front-line employees, and to consider the priorities and direction of the organization.

- **We change the format of our top leadership meetings;** no more sitting at a table listening to readouts from slides on progress but instead walking the room to talk about priorities, reacting to real working prototypes, creating our own prioritized list of actions, solving our greatest impediments.

- **We act as catalysts** in the transformation process.

- **We embrace symbolic changes:** abandoning corner offices for a shared table in the middle of the building where we are accessible to everyone, giving up assigned parking places and turning them over to client visitors, conducting weekly get-togethers in the company café to provide business updates and answer questions, openly admitting what is going well and what needs more attention.

- **We publicize our commitment** to changing our own behaviors and will share our personal development agenda.

- **We seek help** in terms of coaching and feedback to change.

As this long list of commitments suggests, leading an agile transition is a lot of work. The agile transition process is not a costly distraction; it *is* the way the business will run. The agile leadership team learns to operate as an agile team in service of its external and internal customers.

Appendix B

DEFINITIONS OF OPERATING MODEL COMPONENTS

Purpose and values: An agile enterprise's purpose is its enduring mission to make an impact; its values express the shared, long-lasting beliefs that guide the agile enterprise's decisions and priorities.

Strategy: An agile enterprise strategy defines the organization's sources of value, where to play, how to win, and the capabilities required to achieve its enduring purpose.

Leadership and culture: In agile enterprises, leaders and the broader organization alike embrace agile values to visibly shift their ways of working to be more customer obsessed, collaborative, and comfortable with adaptation.

- *Leadership:* Leadership mindsets and behaviors shift to trusting and coaching instead of predicting and controlling, and senior executives collaborate as an agile strategy team.

- *Culture:* Agile values are embedded throughout the organization through peoples' mindsets, behaviors, and routines, creating a culture of collaboration and innovation.

Planning, budgeting, and reviewing: Agile enterprises use a more frequent, more flexible *management system* to dynamically focus resources on the most valuable opportunities. The cycle starts with defining strategic priorities; supporting those priorities with people and dollars; and then measuring the results of the priorities based on financial, customer, and employee impact. Results metrics feed back into strategic prioritization to inform where to continue, pivot, or stop work.

- *Planning:* In a dynamic process, agile enterprises create hypotheses of the most valuable opportunities for the organization to test and determine when and how best to pursue them.

- *Budgeting:* Agile enterprises use a frequent, flexible, venture capital–style approach to funding strategic priorities: testing, learning, and reallocating dollars to where they can have the most impact.

- *Reviewing:* Agile enterprises create feedback loops and have candid performance dialogues. They use simple, transparent metrics and cascade them through the organization to track actual versus expected performance and to adapt approaches.

Structure and accountabilities: Structure and accountabilities in the agile enterprise reflect both the boundaries and roles of business units and the more granular view of team composition and individual decision rights.

- *Organizational units:* An agile enterprise aligns its business units to the sources of value in the organization, and it defines clear ownership across the matrix of business units, functions, and the center.

- *Teams and jobs:* Agile enterprises map the work that needs to be done to meet customer needs and deploy dedicated cross-functional agile teams to change the business. Agile enterprises create jobs that empower individuals with defined decision rights to make rapid progress.

Talent engine: An agile enterprise's talent engine defines both what talent is needed—the capabilities and skills required to support strategic priorities—and how the talent strategy will be achieved with a fast-moving, performance-driven talent system.

- *Talent strategy:* Agile enterprises establish multiyear people priorities for how to hire and retain the best. The talent strategy defines the skills and competencies required to achieve business goals and the balance of internal and external sourcing that will best drive results.

- *Talent system:* Agile enterprises use performance-driven processes for determining how to acquire, deploy, assess, develop, reward, and inspire talent, and continuously improve the systems and approaches to people management.

Business processes: Agile enterprises use business processes as enablers to deliver great customer solutions. Business processes are simple and are constantly improving. They integrate individuals, teams, data, and technology to deliver disruptive innovation or repeatability where needed, across functions.

Technology and data: Technology and data in an agile enterprise include the hardwiring of modular architecture, continuous delivery processes, and data quality, as well as the soft wiring of capabilities and ways of working to enable rapid decision making and collaboration across business and technology.

- *Technology:* Agile enterprises embrace modular, flexible, and service-oriented architectures with effective DevOps and automation to enable continuous delivery, and tools and ways of working to support effective collaboration.

- *Data:* Agile enterprises create and capture high-value data to improve the speed, quality, and cost of making decisions. They also establish modern architectures to provide access to data.

RESEARCH NOTES SUMMARY

Agile is popular and intuitively appealing, but those aren't valid reasons to embrace it. Agile operates on empiricism, the philosophy that all hypotheses should be tested with empirical evidence. Companies deciding whether to try agile should look beyond inspirational anecdotes to unbiased, broad-based evidence on whether it works and how to improve the odds of success. Companies that are succeeding with agile pilots should probably examine the evidence on whether further scaling of agile tends to help or hurt results. Companies that are struggling to make agile work are likely to wonder: Is the problem with us, or are other companies also having similar problems with agile approaches? Bain & Company has been collecting and analyzing data on agile approaches for several years in order to objectively and confidently answer five key questions:

1. Does increasing and improving innovation actually improve business results?

2. Does agile innovation produce better results than traditional innovation methods?

3. Do benefits persist when agile is scaled across many teams?

4. Do benefits persist when agile is applied beyond technology departments?

5. Do agile enterprises improve results?

We collected seventy third-party research reports, including journal articles, books, government papers, academic theses, conference papers, consultancy research, and corporate research. The studies included highly rigorous ongoing studies and metastudies, as well as more limited, point-in-time surveys. We analyzed each report's findings on the relationship between innovation and business outcomes and cataloged findings across the five concepts above as "relationship found," "no relationship found," or "inconclusive." We will continue to expand and update our database with additional research reports as we identify relevant research.

We found strong support between innovation and business outcomes across the five concepts we tested, with very strong support for "innovation improves business results, broadly," and "agile enterprises improve results."

1. Ninety-two percent of reports showed that innovation does improve business results, broadly, with 8 percent of reports inconclusive.

2. Seventy-six percent of reports showed that agile innovation is better than regular innovation, with 10 percent of reports disagreeing and 14 percent of reports inconclusive.

3. Sixty-seven percent of reports showed that benefits persist when agile is scaled across many teams, with 4 percent of reports disagreeing and 29 percent of reports inconclusive.

4. Eighty-one percent of reports showed that benefits persist when agile is applied outside of IT, with 19 percent of reports inconclusive.

5. One hundred percent of reports showed that agile enterprises improve results, although the evidence base is mostly nonacademic, likely reflecting the early stage of research in this emerging area.

So far, this empirical data is very encouraging. Nevertheless, it is not 100 percent positive, and it can change. We recommend that you examine the data for yourself. Study the details of the research, understand the methodologies, and track results as further research pours in—as companies use agile approaches in different places, in different ways, and for longer time periods. Listed below you will find our current compilation of seventy third-party reports addressing the five key questions, along with the findings from each one.

Works Cited

Innovation Improves Business Results, Broadly

Relationship Found

Atalay, Murat, Nilgün Anafarta, and Fulya Sarvan. "The Relationship between Innovation and Firm Performance: An Empirical Evidence from Turkish Automotive Supplier Industry." *Procedia—Social and Behavioral Sciences* 75 (April 3, 2013): 226–235. https://doi.org/10.1016/j.sbspro.2013.04.026.

> Product and process innovation positively and significantly affected firm performance.

Australian Bureau of Statistics. "Innovation in Australian Business, 2016–17." Australian Bureau of Statistics. Updated July 19, 2018. http://www.abs.gov.au/ausstats/abs@.nsf/0/06B08353E0EABA96CA25712A001 61216?Opendocument.

> Innovative businesses reported increased revenues, felt they gained a competitive edge, and had improved customer service.

Cho, Hee-Jae, and Vladimir Pucik. "Relationship between Innovativeness, Quality, Growth, Profitability, and Market Value." *Strategic Management Journal* 26 (April 11, 2005): 555–575. https://doi.org/10.1002/smj.461.

Results show innovativeness mediates the relationship between quality and growth, quality mediates the relationship between innovativeness and profitability, and both innovativeness and quality have mediation effects on market value.

Jiménez-Jiménez, Daniel, and Raquel Sanz-Valle. "Innovation, Organizational Learning, and Performance." *Journal of Business Research* 64, no. 4 (April 2011): 408–417. https://doi.org/10.1016/j.jbusres.2010.09.010.

Study shows that organizational learning and innovation contribute positively to business performance.

Kelly, Bryan, Dimitris Papanikolaou, Amit Seru, and Matt Taddy. "Measuring Technological Innovation over the Long Run." NBER Working Paper No. 25266, National Bureau of Economic Research, Inc., Cambridge, MA (November 2018). https://www.nber.org/papers/w25266.

Breakthrough innovations corresponded with increased productivity across time periods, industries, and firms.

Linder, Jane C. "Does Innovation Drive Profitable Growth? New Metrics for a Complete Picture." *Journal of Business Strategy* 27, no. 5 (September 1, 2006): 38–44. https://doi.org/10.1108/02756660610692699.

Ranking based on financial data corresponds well to executives' self-reported information about how innovative their organizations are.

Minor, Dylan, Paul Brook, and Josh Bernoff. "Are Innovative Companies More Profitable?" *MIT Sloan Management Review*, December 28, 2017. https://sloanreview.mit.edu/article/are-innovative-companies-more-profitable/.

Study found a significant correlation between the ideation rate at companies and growth in profit or net income.

Nieves, Julia. "Outcomes of Management Innovation: An Empirical Analysis in the Services Industry." *European Management Review* 13 (March 21, 2016): 125–136. https://doi.org/10.1111/emre.12071.

Management innovation has a positive influence on product innovation and product innovation has a significant influence on financial performance.

Rajapathirana, R. P. Jayani, and Yan Hui. "Relationship between Innovation Capability, Innovation Type, and Firm Performance." *Journal of Innovation & Knowledge* 3, no. 1 (January–April 2018): 44–55. https://doi.org/10.1016/j.jik.2017.06.002.

Study supports assertion that companies with higher innovation capabilities are influenced positively and very strongly.

Shanker, Roy, Ramudu Bhanugopan, Beatrice I. J. M. van der Heijden, and Mark Farrell. "Organizational Climate for Innovation and Organizational Performance: The Mediating Effect of Innovative Work Behavior." *Journal of Vocational Behavior* 100 (June 2017): 67–77. https://doi.org/10.1016/j.jvb.2017.02 .004.

Study shows that the relationship between organizational climate for innovation and organizational performance is significant.

Inconclusive

Youtie, Jan, Philip Shapira, and Stephen Roper. "Exploring Links between Innovation and Profitability in Georgia Manufacturers." *Economic Development Quarterly* 32, no. 4 (September 3, 2018): 271–287. https://doi.org/10.1177 /0891242418786430.

Positive relationship between profitability and innovation in Georgia manufacturing in the 2005 survey, but no connection between innovation and firm performance in the 2010 and 2016 surveys.

Agile Innovation Is Even Better Than Regular Innovation

Relationship Found

Ambler, Scott W. "2013 IT Project Success Rates Survey Results." Ambysoft, January 2014. http://www.ambysoft.com/surveys/success2013.html.

Agile, lean, and iterative strategies were superior on average to traditional and ad hoc strategies.

CollabNet VersionOne. *13th Annual State of Agile Report*. State of Agile, May 7, 2019. https://www.stateofagile.com/?_ga=2.258734218.1293249604 .1571223036-453094266.1571223036#ufh-c-473508-state-of-agile-report.

Reported benefits of agile include ability to manage changing priorities, project visibility, business/IT alignment, time to market, increased productivity, and reduced project risk.

Fitzgerald, Brian, Gerard Hartnett, and Kieran Conboy. "Customising Agile Methods to Software Practices at Intel Shannon." *European Journal of Information Systems* 15, no. 2 (January 9, 2006): 200–213. https://doi.org/10.1057 /palgrave.ejis.3000605.

Study investigated tailoring of the agile methods, eXtreme programming (XP), and Scrum, at Intel Shannon. Benefits included reductions in code defect density by a factor of 7 and faster project delivery.

Freeform Dynamics. *How Agile and DevOps Enable Digital Readiness and Transformation.* Freeform Dynamics, February 2018. https://freeformdynamics .com/software-delivery/agile-devops-enable-digital-readiness-transformation/.

On average, agility masters reported 60 percent higher revenue growth and were 2.4 times more likely than peers to be growing at over 20 percent.

Johnson, Suzette, Richard Cheng, Stosh Misiazek, Stephanie Greytak, and James Boston. *The Business Case for Agile Methods.* Arlington, VA: Association for Enterprise Information, 2011. http://docplayer.net/5838794-The-business-case-for -agile-methods.html.

Patriot Excalibur (PEX) software release cycle decreased from eighteen months to twenty-two weeks; BMC adoption of agile led to individual team productivity increases of 20 to 50 percent; adoption of agile helped US Census Bureau deliver mandated requirements 50 percent faster using a third of the staff of previous efforts.

Kakar, Adarsh K. "What Motivates Team Members and Users of Agile Projects?" *Proceedings of the Southern Association for Information Systems Conference* 17. Atlanta: Association for Information Systems (AIS), 2013. https://aisel.aisnet.org /sais2013/17.

Agile methods enhance the completion effect of project team members, motivating them to work toward completing the project.

Lo Giudice, Diego, Christopher Mines, Amanda LeClair, Luis Deya, and Andrew Reese. *The State of Agile 2017: Agile at Scale.* Forrester, December 14, 2017. https://www.forrester.com/report/The+State+Of+Agile+2017+Agile+At+Scale/-/E -RES140411.

Benefits of agile include greater frequency of releases, improved customer experience, better business/IT alignment, improved functional quality, and higher team morale.

Przybilla, Leonard, Manuel Wiesche, and Helmut Krcmar. "The Influence of Agile Practices on Performance in Software Engineering Teams: A Subgroup Perspective." In *Proceedings of the 2018 ACM SIGMIS Conference on Computers and People Research*, 33–40. New York: Association for Computing Machinery, June 2018. https://doi.org/10.1145/3209626.3209703.

Daily stand-ups and retrospectives reduced levels of conflict and increased performance and satisfaction.

Reifer, Donald J. "How Good Are Agile Methods?" *IEEE Software* 19, no. 4 (2002): 16–18. https://doi.org/10.1109/MS.2002.1020280.

> Benefits included improved productivity improvement (15–23 percent), cost reduction (5–7 percent), and time-to-market compression (25–50 percent).

Rico, David F. "What Is the Return on Investment (ROI) of Agile Methods?" Semantic Scholar. Accessed December 17, 2019. https://pdfs.semanticscholar.org/8e3d/c7208bc743037716f327ba98a7fcb1a69502.pdf.

> Based on literature examined, use of agile methods results in increased cost-effectiveness, productivity, quality, cycle-time reduction, and customer satisfaction.

Scrum Alliance. *State of Scrum 2017–18 Report*. ScrumAlliance. Accessed December 17, 2019. https://www.scrumalliance.org/learn-about-scrum/state-of-scrum.

> Ninety-seven percent of participants will continue to use Scrum in the future. Benefits of agile adoption include improved satisfaction with what gets delivered, better time to market, better quality, improved staff morale, and improved return on investment in IT.

Serrador, Pedro, Andrew Gemino, and Blaize H. Reich. "Creating a Climate for Project Success." *Journal of Modern Project Management* 6 (2018): 38–47. https://doi.org/10.19255/JMPM01604.

> Senior management support, stakeholder engagement, fully dedicated teams, support for agile methods, frequent meetings with product owners, and a good team attitude related to project success.

Serrador, Pedro, and Jeffrey K. Pinto. "Does Agile Work? A Quantitative Analysis of Agile Project Success." *International Journal of Project Management* 33, no. 5 (July 1, 2015): 1040–1051. https://doi.org/10.1016/j.ijproman.2015.01.006.

> Agile methods have a positive impact on efficiency and overall stakeholder satisfaction.

Standish Group. *CHAOS Report: Decision Latency Theory: It's All about the Interval*. Boston: Lulu.com, 2018. https://www.standishgroup.com/store/.

> Agile projects are three-fifths more likely to succeed (42.5 percent vs. 26 percent) and one-third as likely to fail (8 percent vs. 21 percent).

No Relationship Found

Budzier, Alexander, and Bent Flyvbjerg. "Making Sense of the Impact and Importance of Outliers in Project Management through the Use of Power Laws." In *Proceedings of International Research Network on Organizing by Projects at Oslo* 11 (June 1, 2013). New York: SSRN, 2016. https://ssrn.com/abstract=2289549.

The group adopting more agile methodologies did not significantly differ in their median cost, schedule, or benefits performance.

Magazinius, Ana, and Robert Feldt. "Confirming Distortional Behaviors in Software Cost Estimation Practice." In *Proceedings of the 37th EUROMICRO Conference on Software Engineering and Advanced Applications*, 411–418. Institute of Electronics and Electronics Engineers, November 3, 2011. https://doi.org/10.1109/SEAA.2011.61.

Examined the variation between agile and nonagile companies and found that the success in meeting time and budget goals and the causes of failures was not significantly different between the two methodologies.

Inconclusive

Dybå, Tore, and Torgeir Dingsøyr. "Empirical Studies of Agile Software Development: A Systematic Review." *Information and Software Technology* 50, nos. 9–10 (August 2008): 833–859. https://doi.org/10.1016/j.infsof.2008.01.006.

Four studies showed a 42 percent increase in productivity for the agile team compared to traditional, but quality of the studies was low.

Eveleens, Johan, and Chris Verhoef. "The Rise and Fall of the Chaos Report Figures." *IEEE Software* 27, no. 1 (January–February 2010): 30–36. https://doi.org/10.1109/MS.2009.154.

Criticizes the Standish chaos report methodology, a frequently cited report on the benefits of agile.

Lindvall, Mikael, Vic Basili, Barry Boehm, Patricia Costa, Kathleen Dangle, Forrest Shull, Roseanne Tesoriero, et al. "Empirical Findings in Agile Methods." In *Extreme Programming and Agile Methods—XP/Agile Universe 2002*, 197–207. Berlin: Springer, 2002. https://doi.org/10.1007/3-540-45672-4_19.

Benefits to adopting agile included improvements in customer collaboration, handling defects, and estimation. Limitations included perceived inefficiency of pair programming and lack of attention to design and architectural issues.

Benefits Persist When Agile Is Scaled across Many Teams

Relationship Found

Atlas, Alan. "Accidental Adoption: The Story of Scrum at Amazon.com." In *Agile 2009 Conference*, 135–140. Institute of Electronics and Electronics Engineers, September 25, 2009. https://doi.org/10.1109/AGILE.2009.10.

From 2004 to 2009, Scrum spread to a large portion of the software development teams at Amazon. Key success factors for adoption included culture, small team size, internal champions, and training.

Brown, Alan W. "A Case Study in Agile-at-Scale Delivery." In *Agile Processes in Software Engineering and Extreme Programming. XP 2011. Lecture Notes in Business Information Processing* 77, 266–291. Berlin: Springer, 2011. https://doi .org/10.1007/978-3-642-20677-1_19.

Describes scaling agile at a bank. Initial eight pilots showed improvements in productivity and quality.

Fry, Chris, and Steve Greene. "Large Scale Agile Transformation in an On-Demand World." In *AGILE 2007*, 136–142. Institute of Electronics and Electronics Engineers, August 27, 2007. https://doi.org/10.1109/AGILE.2007.38.

Describes Salesforce.com's adoption of agile at scale. In an organizational survey, 80 percent believe that the new development methodology is making their team more effective.

Furuhjelm, Jörgen, Johan Segertoft, Joe Justice, and J. J. Sutherland. "Owning the Sky with Agile." Global Scrum Gathering, San Diego, California, April 10–12, 2017. https://www.scruminc.com/wp-content/uploads/2015/09/Release-version _Owning-the-Sky-with-Agile.pdf.

Through scaling agile, Saab Defense delivered aircraft at lower cost, with higher speed, and with greater quality.

Jørgensen, Magne. "Do Agile Methods Work for Large Software Projects?" In *Agile Processes in Software Engineering and Extreme Programming. XP 2018. Lecture Notes in Business Information Processing* 314: 179–190. Cham, Switzerland: Springer, 2018. https://doi.org/10.1007/978-3-319-91602-6_12.

Projects using agile methods performed on average much better than those using nonagile methods for medium and large software projects.

Kalenda, Martin, Petr Hyna, and Bruno Rossi. "Scaling Agile in Large Organizations: Practices, Challenges, and Success Factors. *Journal of Software: Evolution and Process* 30, no. 10 (May 16, 2018). https://doi.org/10.1002/smr.1954.

Global software company succeeded in scaling agile by tailoring the process to the needs of the company, maintaining an agile mindset, and having experienced agile team members.

Knaster, R., and D. Leffingwell. *SAFe 4.0 Distilled: Applying the Scaled Agile Framework for Lean Software and Systems Engineering.* Boston: Addison-Wesley, 2017.

Cites various companies achieving improvements in quality, productivity, employee engagement, faster time to market, program execution, alignment, and transparency by adopting Scaled Agile Framework (SAFe) to scale agile.

Korhonen, Kirsi. "Evaluating the Impact of an Agile Transformation: A Longitudinal Case Study in a Distributed Context." *Software Quality Journal* 21 (November 1, 2012): 599–624. https://doi.org/10.1007/s11219-012-9189-4.

Nokia Siemens Networks increased visibility, increased ability to react to changes in requirements, improved quality of the software development, and increased employee motivation.

Lagerberg, Lina, Tor Skude, Pär Emanuelsson, Kristian Sandahl, and Daniel Ståhl. "The Impact of Agile Principles and Practices on Large-Scale Software Development Projects: A Multiple-Case Study of Two Projects at Ericsson." In *2013 ACM / IEEE International Symposium on Empirical Software Engineering and Measurement*, 348–356. Institute of Electronics and Electronics Engineers, December 12, 2013. https://doi.org/10.1109/ESEM.2013.53.

Implementation of agile was found to contribute to knowledge sharing, correlate with increased project visibility and coordination effectiveness, and possibly increased productivity.

Paasivaara, Maria, Benjamin Behm, Casper Lassenius, and Minna Hallikainen. "Large-Scale Agile Transformation at Ericsson: A Case Study." *Empirical Software Engineering* 23 (January 11, 2018): 2550–2596. https://doi.org/10.1007/s10664-017-9555-8.

Describes how Ericsson introduced agile in a new R&D product development program while simultaneously scaling it up aggressively. Key success factors included having an agile mindset, making gradual changes (vs. big bang), and customizing the scaling method to the company.

Schnitter, Joachim, and Olaf Mackert. "Large-Scale Agile Software Development at SAP AG." In *Evaluation of Novel Approaches to Software Engineering. Communications in Computer and Information Science*, 209–220. Berlin: Springer, 2011. https://doi.org/10.1007/978-3-642-23391-3_15.

SAP scaled agile to 18,000 developers in twelve global locations. Though implementation was difficult, agile significantly improved transparency and informal communication.

Vaidya, Aashish. "Does DAD Know Best, Is It Better to Do LeSS or Just Be SAFe? Adapting Scaling Agile Practices into the Enterprise." Presented at the Pacific Northwest Software Quality Conference, Portland, OR, October 20–22, 2014. http://www.uploads.pnsqc.org/2014/Papers/t-033_Vaidya_paper.pdf.

Cambia Health Solutions rolled out Scrum and other agile practices across more than forty teams. Benefits include improved delivery process and quality practices.

Inconclusive

Bjarnason, Elizabeth, Krzysztof Wnuk, and Björn Regnell. "A Case Study on Benefits and Side-Effects of Agile Practices in Large-Scale Requirements Engineering." In *Proceedings of the 1st Agile Requirements Engineering Workshop*, 1–5. New York: ACM, 2011. https://doi.org/10.1145/2068783.2068786.

Results indicate that agile practices (at least partly) remedy several challenges and issues related to traditional requirements engineering in large-scale software development, though they also pose new challenges.

Conboy, Kieran, and Noel Carroll. "Implementing Large-Scale Agile Frameworks: Challenges and Recommendations." *IEEE Software* 36, no. 2 (March–April 2019): 44–50. https://doi.org/10.1109/MS.2018.2884865.

Describes challenges to scaling agile and offers recommendations to mitigate them.

Dikert, Kim, Maria Paasivaara, and Casper Lassenius. "Challenges and Success Factors for Large-Scale Agile Transformations: A Systematic Literature Review." *Journal of Systems and Software* 119 (September 2016): 87–108. https://doi.org/10.1016/j.jss.2016.06.013.

Identifies challenges and success factors for large-scale agile transformations.

Moe, Nils, Bjørn Dahl, Viktoria Stray, Lina Sund Karlsen, and Stine Schjødt-Osmo. "Team Autonomy in Large-Scale Agile." ScholarSpace, January 8, 2019. https://doi.org/10.24251/HICSS.2019.839.

Identified barriers to team autonomy when scaling agile and suggested ways to mitigate them.

Paasivaara, Maria. "Adopting SAFe to Scale Agile in a Globally Distributed Organization." In *Proceedings of 2017 IEEE 12th International Conference on Global Software Engineering*, 36–40. Institute of Electronics and Electronics Engineers, July 17, 2017. https://doi.org/10.1109/ICGSE.2017.15.

Describes how Comptel, a globally distributed software development company, adopted the SAFe framework in two business lines. The second business line was more successful due to learnings from the first business.

Paasivaara, Maria, and Casper Lassenius. "Scaling Scrum in a Large Globally Distributed Organization: A Case Study." In *2016 IEEE 11th International Conference on Global Software Engineering*, 74–83. Institute of Electronics and Electronics Engineers, September 29, 2016. https://doi.org/10.1109/ICGSE.2016.34.

Commercially, agile transformation was a success, but team lacked agile mindset, did not adopt all important practices suggested by the LeSS framework, and interteam coordination was insufficient.

Paasivaara, Maria, Casper Lassenius, and Ville T. Heikkilä. "Inter-Team Coordination in Large-Scale Globally Distributed Scrum: Do Scrum-of-Scrums Really Work?" In *Proceedings of the 2012 ACM-IEEE International Symposium on Empirical Software Engineering and Measurement*, 236–238. New York: ACM, 2012. https://doi.org/10.1145/2372251.2372294.

> Scrum-of-Scrum meetings involving representatives from all teams were severely challenged. Interteam meetings where participants have joint goals and interests were more effective.

Agile Works beyond IT

Relationship Found

CMG Partners. *Sixth Annual CMO's Agenda: The Agile Advantage*. CMOs Agenda, 2013. https://cmosagenda.com/always-always-agile.

> Benefits of adopting agile in marketing include improved speed, ability to adapt, productivity, prioritization, and ability to deliver customer-centric outcomes.

Fryrear, Andrea. "State of Agile Marketing." AgileSherpas. Accessed December 18, 2019. https://www.agilesherpas.com/state-of-agile-marketing-2019/.

> Thirty-two percent of participants are adopting at least some parts of agile methodologies in marketing; 50 percent plan to adopt agile in the next year. Benefits include ability to adapt, improved quality, and faster speed.

Furuhjelm, Jörgen, Johan Segertoft, Joe Justice, and J. J. Sutherland. "Owning the Sky with Agile." Global Scrum Gathering, San Diego, California, April 10–12, 2017. https://www.scruminc.com/wp-content/uploads/2015/09/Release-version_Owning-the-Sky-with-Agile.pdf.

> Saab Defense has adopted an agile process to address the issue in both hardware and software teams to produce a new multirole strike fighter, the JAS 39E Saab Gripen. It was delivered at lower cost, with higher speed, and greater quality.

McFarland, Keith R. "Should You Build Strategy Like You Build Software?" *MIT Sloan Management Review* 49, no. 3 (2009): 69–74. https://sloanreview.mit.edu/article/should-you-build-strategy-like-you-build-software/.

> Shamrock Foods Company, a food distributor, successfully implemented a spiral planning model, an agile approach to strategic planning.

Petrini, Stefano, and Jorge Muniz Jr. "Scrum Management Approach Applied in Aerospace Sector." Presented at the IIE Annual Conference, Montreal, Canada, May 31–June 3, 2014.

The adoption of Scrum in system testing of aircraft parts showed improved efficiency, adaptability, visibility, and employee motivation.

Raubenolt, Amy. "An Analysis of Collaborative Problem-Solving Mechanisms in Sponsored Projects: Applying the 5-Day Sprint Model." *Journal of Research Administration* 47, no. 2 (2016): 94–111. https://files.eric.ed.gov/fulltext /EJ1152255.pdf.

The Office of Finance and Sponsored Projects at the Research Institute at Nationwide Children's Hospital conducted a five-day design sprint session to redesign a reporting process. The sprint feedback was overwhelmingly positive: all teams indicated they would recommend the sprint model to solve future problems.

Scheuermann, Constantin, Stephan Verclas, and Bernd Bruegge. "Agile Factory—An Example of an Industry 4.0 Manufacturing Process." In *2015 IEEE 3rd International Conference on Cyber-Physical Systems, Networks, and Applications*, 43–47. Institute of Electronics and Electronics Engineers, September 21, 2015. https://doi.org/10.1109/CPSNA.2015.17.

Describes the successful development of an Agile Factory prototype to transfer agile software engineering techniques to the domain of manufacturing.

Serrador, Pedro, and Jeffrey K. Pinto. "Does Agile Work?—A Quantitative Analysis of Agile Project Success." *International Journal of Project Management* 33, no. 5 (July 2015): 1040–1051. https://doi.org/10.1016/j.ijproman.2015.01.006.

Data sample of 1,002 projects across multiple industries, countries, and project types showed that the greater the agile/iterative approach reported, the higher the reported project success.

Skinner, Ryan, Mary Pilecki, Melissa Parrish, Lori Wizdo, Jessica Liu, Chahiti Asarpota, and Christine Turley. *Agile Methodology Embeds Customer Obsession in Marketing*. Forrester, July 1, 2019. https://www.forrester.com/report/Agile+Me thodology+Embeds+Customer+Obsession+In+Marketing/-/E-RES139938.

Provides examples of companies adopting agile principles and practices in marketing. Benefits include improved focus, speed to market, ability to respond to change, and realism about team capacity.

Sommer, Anita Friis, Christian Hedegaard, Iskra Dukovska-Popovska, and Kenn Steger-Jensen. "Improved Product Development Performance through Agile/Stage-Gate Hybrids: The Next-Generation Stage-Gate Process?" *Research-Technology Management* 58 (December 28, 2015): 34–45. https://doi.org/10 .5437/08956308X5801236.

The five companies that implemented Agile/Stage-Gate hybrids reported significant positive effects including improved efficiencies, reduced process iterations, improved visibility, better defined goals, decreased customer complaints, increased team ownership and morale.

Sutherland, Jeff, and J. J. Sutherland. *Scrum: The Art of Doing Twice the Work in Half the Time*. New York: Crown Business, 2014.

> Provides examples of companies successfully adopting Scrum in various functions and industries. For example, Scrum was deployed in schools in the Netherlands resulting in a 10 percent improvement in test scores.

van Solingen, Rini, Jeff Sutherland, and Denny de Waard. "Scrum in Sales: How to Improve Account Management and Sales Processes." In *Agile 2011 Conference*, 284–288. Institute of Electronics and Electronics Engineers, August 20, 2011. https://doi.org/10.1109/AGILE.2011.12.

> Benefits of adopting Scrum in sales and account management included increased revenue, team self-motivation, and predictability of sales.

Willeke, Marian H. H. "Agile in Academics: Applying Agile to Instructional Design." In *Agile 2011 Conference*, 246–251. Institute of Electronics and Electronics Engineers, August 30, 2011. https://doi.org/10.1109/AGILE.2011.17.

> Applying agile to curriculum design increased productivity and employee motivation.

Inconclusive

Ahmed-Kristensen, Saeema, and Jaap Daalhuizen. "Pioneering the Combined Use of Agile and Stage-Gate Models in New Product Development—Cases from the Manufacturing Industry." *Proceedings of Innovation & Product Development Management Conference*, Copenhagen, Denmark, June 14–16, 2015. https://pdfs.semanticscholar.org/a53d/1f7909c01c8626b8da9dfa5ae7214f6e658b.pdf.

> Agile enabled faster identification of the need to change a requirement, and improved informal knowledge sharing. Challenges included understanding how to remain agile and welcome changes in design requirements while adhering to strict regulations.

Agile Enterprises Can Improve Results

Relationship Found

Appelbaum, Steven, Rafael Calla, Dany Desautels, and Lisa N. Hasan. "The Challenges of Organizational Agility: Part 2." *Industrial and Commercial Training* 49, no. 2 (February 6, 2017): 69–74. https://doi.org/10.1108/ICT-05-2016-0028.

> Organizational agility enables employees to respond proactively to unexpected environmental changes, but it's difficult. It requires changes in leadership, decision-making dynamics, skills, and interpersonal relationships.

Business Agility Institute. *2019 Business Agility Report: Raising the B.A.R.*, 2nd ed. Business Agility Institute. https://businessagility.institute/learn/2019 -business-agility-report-raising-the-bar/.

> Reported benefits from business agility include increased customer satisfaction, greater employee satisfaction, and improved market performance.

Denning, S. *The Age of Agile: How Smart Companies Are Transforming the Way Work Gets Done.* New York: AMACOM, 2018.

> Provides examples of agile enterprises (or companies on the path to becoming agile enterprises) and their success due to improved quality, innovation, and speed-to-market.

Glenn, Marie. *Organisational Agility: How Business Can Survive and Thrive in Turbulent Times.* Economist Intelligence Unit, CFO Innovation, March 1, 2010. https://www.cfoinnovation.com/organisational-agility-how-business-can-survive -and-thrive-turbulent-times.

> Nearly 90 percent of executives surveyed believe that organizational agility is critical for business success. Cites research suggesting agile firms grow revenue 37 percent faster and generate 30 percent higher profits than nonagile companies.

Project Management Institute. "Achieving Greater Agility: The People and Process Drivers that Accelerate Results." Project Management Institute, September 2017. https://www.pmi.org/learning/thought-leadership/pulse/agile-project.

> Organizations with high agility report more projects meet original goals and business intent; experience more revenue growth, with 75 percent reporting a minimum of 5 percent year-over-year; and are more likely to execute on critical people and process drivers.

Saha, Nibedita, Ales Gregar, and Petr Sáha. "Organizational Agility and HRM Strategy: Do They Really Enhance Firms' Competitiveness?" *International Journal of Organizational Leadership* 6 (2017): 323–334. https://doi.org/10.33844 /ijol.2017.60454.

> Study suggests increased awareness (sensing agility), responsiveness (decision– making agility), and organization promptness (acting agility) promote individual competence, organizational learning, and organizational innovativeness.

Sutherland, J. J. *The Scrum Fieldbook: A Master Class on Accelerating Performance, Getting Results, and Defining the Future.* New York: Currency, 2019.

> Describes examples and the benefits of becoming a Renaissance enterprise, a company that scales Scrum throughout the organization.

Yang, Chyan, and Hsian-Ming Liu. "Boosting Firm Performance via Enterprise Agility and Network Structure." *Management Decision* 50 (June 22, 2012): 1022–1044. https://doi.org/10.1108/00251741211238319.

Results show that a firm's agility capability and its network structure are critical to firm performance. In addition, firms with superior enterprise agility are better able to exploit the network structure.

Inconclusive

Ries, Eric. *The Startup Way: How Modern Companies Use Entrepreneurial Management to Transform Culture and Drive Long-Term Growth.* New York: Currency, 2017.

Provides examples of companies adopting agile and entrepreneurial principles across their organization to grow revenue and drive innovation; however, GE, a prominent example in the book, has faced historic stock decline since adopting lean start-up practices.

Notes

Introduction

1. Of 101,592 international surveyed software developers, 85.9 percent use agile in their work. "Developer Survey Results, 2018," Stack Overflow, https://insights.stackoverflow.com/survey/2018#development-practices (accessed December 9, 2019).

2. Sears Holdings, "Sears Holdings Outlines Next Phase of Its Strategic Transformation," press release, February 10, 2017, https://searsholdings.com/press-releases/pr/2030.

3. See Weber's classic work *The Protestant Ethic and the Spirit of Capitalism.* One recent edition was published by Routledge Classics (Oxford and New York, 2001).

4. Frederick Winslow Taylor, *The Principles of Scientific Management* (New York: Harper & Brothers, 1911). Also available from Project Gutenberg.

5. See Dominic Barton, Dennis Carey, and Ram Charan, "One Bank's Agile Team Experiment," *Harvard Business Review*, March–April 2018, 59–61.

6. Anthony Mersino, "Agile Project Success Rates 2X Higher than Traditional Projects (2019)," Vitality Chicago, April 1, 2018, https://vitalitychicago.com/blog/agile-projects-are-more-successful-traditional-projects/.

Chapter 1

1. Hirotaka Takeuchi and Ikujiro Nonaka, "The New New Product Development Game," *Harvard Business Review*, January–February 1986, 137–146.

2. Takeuchi and Nonaka, "The New New Product Development Game," 137.

3. James O. Coplien, "Borland Software Craftsmanship: A New Look at Process, Quality and Productivity," in *Proceedings of the 5th Annual Borland International Conference*, Orlando, Florida, June 5, 1994, https://pdfs.semanticscholar.org/3a09/1c3f265de024b18ccbf88a6aead223133e39.pdf.

4. Steven L. Goldman, Roger N. Nagel, and Kenneth Preiss, *Agile Competitors and Virtual Organizations: Strategies for Enriching the Customer* (New York: John Wiley, 1994).

5. The agile manifesto is available at https://agilemanifesto.org/ (accessed December 30, 2019).

6. Darrell K. Rigby, Jeff Sutherland, and Hirotaka Takeuchi, "Embracing Agile: How to Master the Process That's Transforming Management," *Harvard Business Review*, May 2016, 40–50.

7. Rigby, Sutherland, and Takeuchi, "Embracing Agile," 42.

Chapter 2

1. Sebastian Wagner, personal interview, 2017.
2. F. Scott Fitzgerald, "The Crack-Up," originally published in *Esquire*, February, March, and April, 1936.
3. Bart Schlatmann and Peter Jacobs, "ING's Agile Transformation," interview by Deepak Mahadevan, *McKinsey Quarterly*, January 2017, https://www .mckinsey.com/industries/financial-services/our-insights/ings-agile-transformation?
4. Tammy Sparrow, phone interviews, November 17 and 27, 2017.
5. See CollabNet VersionOne, *13th Annual State of Agile Report*, May 7, 2019, https://www.stateofagile.com/?_ga=2.211020822.2043163775.1579308446 -1467289744.1577216170#ufh-i-521251909-13th-annual-state-of-agile-report /473508.
6. Henrik Kniberg and Anders Ivarsson, "Scaling Agile @ Spotify with Tribes, Squads, Chapters & Guilds," October 2012, https://blog.crisp.se/wp -content/uploads/2012/11/SpotifyScaling.pdf.

Chapter 3

1. Mark Allen, "Mark Allen Interview on Heart Rate Training and Racing," interview by Floris Gierman, Extramilest, July 2, 2015, https://extramilest.com /blog/mark-allen-interview-on-training-and-racing/.
2. Allen, "Mark Allen Interview."
3. Susan Lacke, "Mark Allen Voted Greatest American Triathlete of All Time," May 7, 2018, Ironman, https://www.ironman.com/news_article/show /1042292.
4. Michael Sheetz, "Technology Killing Off Corporate America: Average Life Span of Companies under 20 Years," *CNBC*, August 24, 2017, https://www.cnbc .com/2017/08/24/technology-killing-off-corporations-average-lifespan-of -company-under-20-years.html; https://www.innosight.com/insight/creative -destruction/.
5. Max Marmer and Ertan Dogrultan, "Startup Genome Report Extra on Premature Scaling," March 2012, https://s3.amazonaws.com/startupcompass -public/StartupGenomeReport2_Why_Startups_Fail_v2.pdf.
6. See, for example, Kate Taylor and Benjamin Goggin, "49 of the Biggest Scandals in Uber's History," *Business Insider*, May 10, 2019, https://www .businessinsider.com/uber-company-scandals-and-controversies-2017-11; Sam Levin, "Uber's Scandals, Blunders and PR Disasters: The Full List," *Guardian*, June 27, 2017, https://www.theguardian.com/technology/2017/jun/18/uber-travis -kalanick-scandal-pr-disaster-timeline.
7. Cadie Thompson, "Elon Musk on Missing Model 3 Production Deadlines," *Business Insider*, December 9, 2018, https://www.businessinsider.com/elon-musk -blames-missed-model-3-production-targets-stupidity-2018-12?nr_email_referer =1&utm_source=Sailthru&utm_medium=email&utm_content=Tech_select.

8. Dan Lovallo and Daniel Kahneman, "Delusions of Success: How Optimism Undermines Executives' Decisions," *Harvard Business Review*, July 2003, 56–63.

9. Dan Gardner and Philip E. Tetlock, *Superforecasting: The Art and Science of Prediction* (New York: Broadway Books, 2016).

10. The mission appears on the company's website: https://www.warbyparker.com/history (accessed January 2, 2020).

11. "Barnes & Noble Mission Statement and/or Vision Statement," http://www.makingafortune.biz/list-of-companies-b/barnes-&-noble.htm (accessed December 10, 2019). Barnes & Noble's website in 2019 seemed to update and simplify this statement: "Barnes & Noble's mission is to operate the best omnichannel specialty retail business in America, helping both our customers and booksellers reach their aspirations, while being a credit to the communities we serve." See https://www.barnesandnobleinc.com/about-bn/ (accessed January 2, 2020).

12. Listing can be found on Wikipedia, s.v. "Ironman World Championship," last modified October 19, 2019, https://en.wikipedia.org/wiki/Ironman_World_Championship.

13. Data from Allen, "Mark Allen Interview."

Chapter 4

1. Daniela Kraemer, phone interview, April 1, 2019.

2. Henk Becker, phone interview, May 2, 2019.

3. See Douglas McGregor, *The Human Side of Enterprise* (New York: McGraw-Hill, 1985). Originally published in 1960.

4. Amar V. Bhidé, *The Origin and Evolution of New Businesses* (New York: Oxford University Press, 2000).

5. Douglas McGregor, *The Professional Manager* (New York: McGraw-Hill, 1967), 163.

6. David Ricardo, *On the Principles of Political Economy and Taxation* (Mineola, NY: Dover, 2004).

7. Anne Kathrin Gebhardt, personal and multiple phone interviews beginning April 15, 2019.

Chapter 5

1. The agile manifesto is available at https://agilemanifesto.org/ (accessed December 30, 2019).

2. Jeff Bezos, "2016 Letter to Shareholders," https://blog.aboutamazon.com/company-news/2016-letter-to-shareholders (accessed January 3, 2020).

3. Darrell K. Rigby, Jeff Sutherland, and Andy Noble, "Agile at Scale," *Harvard Business Review*, May–June 2018, 95.

Chapter 6

1. Alfred D. Chandler Jr., *Strategy and Structure: Chapters in the History of the Industrial Enterprises* (Cambridge, Mass.: MIT Press, 1962), 314.
2. Daniela Kraemer, phone interview, April 1, 2019.
3. "Help Increase the GDP of the Internet," Stripe, https://stripe.com/jobs (accessed January 3, 2020).
4. "A Quick Guide to Stripe's Culture," Stripe, https://stripe.com/jobs /culture (accessed January 6, 2020).
5. Michael Mankins and Eric Garton, *Time, Talent, Energy* (Boston: Harvard Business Review Press, 2017).
6. Henk Becker, phone interview, May 2, 2019.
7. Becker, phone interview.
8. Anne Lis, phone interview, May 2, 2019.
9. Mankins and Garton, *Time, Talent, Energy*, 127.
10. Mankins and Garton, *Time, Talent, Energy*, 120.

Chapter 7

1. Les Matheson, interview, Edinburgh, November 17, 2019.
2. Matheson, interview.
3. Frans Woelders, interview, Edinburgh, November 5, 2019.
4. Elizabeth Swan and Tracy O'Rourke, *The Problem-Solver's Toolkit: A Surprisingly Simple Guide to Your Lean Six Sigma Journey* (Seattle: Amazon Digital Services, 2018).
5. Hongyi Chen and Ryan Taylor, "Exploring the Impact of Lean Management on Innovation Capability," in *Proceedings of PICMET '09—Technology Management in the Age of Fundamental Change*, Portland International Center for Management of Engineering and Technology (New York: Institute of Electrical and Electronics Engineers, 2009), 816–824.
6. Steve Blank, "When Startups Scrapped the Business Plan," interview by Curt Nickisch, *Harvard Business Review*, August 23, 2017, https://hbr.org /ideacast/2017/08/when-startups-scrapped-the-business-plan.html.
7. Eric Ries, *The Lean Startup: How Today's Entrepreneurs Use Continuous Innovation to Create Radically Successful Businesses* (New York: Crown Publishing, 2011), Kindle edition, 4.
8. Marty Cagan, *Inspired: How to Create Tech Products Customers Love* (New York: Wiley, 2017), Kindle edition, 49.

Chapter 8

1. "When a meeting, or part thereof, is held under the Chatham House Rule, participants are free to use the information received, but neither the identity nor the affiliation of the speaker(s), nor that of any other participant, may be

revealed." See "Chatham House Rule," https://www.chathamhouse.org/chatham -house-rule (accessed December 30, 2019).

2. George Anders, "Inside Amazon's Idea Machine: How Bezos Decodes Customers," *Forbes*, April 23, 2012, https://www.forbes.com/sites/georgeanders /2012/04/04/inside-amazon/#1058738b6199.

3. The mission appears on Amazon's website. "Come Build the Future with Us," https://www.amazon.jobs/en/working/working-amazon (accessed December 30, 2019).

4. The principles appear on Amazon's website. "Leadership Principles," https://www.amazon.jobs/en/principles (accessed December 30, 2019).

5. Eugene Kim, "Jeff Bezos to Employees: 'One Day, Amazon Will Fail,' but Our Job Is to Delay It as Long as Possible," CNBC, November 15, 2018, https:// www.cnbc.com/2018/11/15/bezos-tells-employees-one-day-amazon-will-fail-and -to-stay-hungry.html.

6. Jack Welch, "Speed, Simplicity, Self-Confidence: An Interview with Jack Welch," interviewed by Noel Tichy and Ram Charan, *Harvard Business Review*, September–October 1989, 113.

7. Amar V. Bhidé, *The Origin and Evolution of New Businesses* (New York: Oxford University Press, 2000), 61.

8. Fred Wilson, "Why Early Stage Venture Investments Fail," Union Square Ventures (USV), November 30, 2007, https://www.usv.com/writing/2007/11/why -early-stage-venture-investments-fail/.

9. Daniel Kahneman, *Thinking, Fast and Slow* (New York: Farrar, Straus and Giroux, 2013), Kindle edition, 207.

10. Teresa Amabile and Steven J. Kramer, "The Power of Small Wins," *Harvard Business Review*, May 2011, https://hbr.org/2011/05/the-power-of-small -wins.

Index

Note: Figures and tables are indicated by *f* and *t*, respectively.

Acknowledgments

Agile is all about collaborative teamwork, and this book has reinforced just how valuable, inspiring, and fun genuine teamwork can be.

We are grateful for the generous support of so many of our partners and colleagues at Bain & Company. It is impossible to thank every individual who shared his or her time, research, and personal experiences with us. Still, we would be terribly remiss not to mention the contributions of Tareq Barto, Matt Crupi, Imeyen Ebong, Arun Ganti, Josh Hinkel, Darren Johnson, Phil Kleweno, Michael Mankins, Prasad Sulur Narasimhan, Andy Noble, Eduardo Roma, Dan Schwartz, Herman Spruit, Jess Tan, Chuck Whitten, and Chris Zook. We wish to thank all of our practice area and research specialists—especially Annie Howard, Ludovica Mottura, and Kristin Ronan Thorpe—who contributed knowledge and rigorous analysis to support and challenge our work. We are grateful to our internal editorial board: James Allen, Mike Baxter, Eric Garton, Patrick Litre, Will Poindexter, and Erika Serow. These people found time in their already impossible schedules to read early drafts and make them better. We also appreciate the work of Bain's design team, led by Dawn Pomeroy Briggs. And we are extraordinarily thankful to Bain's editorial team—especially John Case, Paul Judge, and Maggie Locher—who spent so much time helping us add clarity and accuracy in our thinking and writing.

We are thankful to Jeff Kehoe and Melinda Merino, our editors at Harvard Business Review Press, for their encouragement to write this book, help in collecting peer feedback from agile experts, and invaluable guidance in refining the manuscript. We also appreciate the assistance of the Press's design expert, Stephani Finks.

We are deeply indebted to the hundreds of agile practitioners who generously, openly, and honestly contributed their experiences to the context and case examples for this book. We regret that client confidentialities and space constraints prevent us from naming each and every one of them. The agile community is a special group of passionate people. They truly exemplify the ideals of the agile manifesto—uncovering better ways of working in agile fashion by doing it and helping others do it. We thank those who participate in Bain's Agile Enterprise Exchange, a group of more than forty senior executives from a wide range of industries, geographies, and business functions who have agreed to meet regularly, network continuously with each other, and openly share insights into their successes and challenges. This exchange is helping agile to become a valuable and sustainable trend. Much of their collective wisdom has shaped this book, and we are grateful to the members who are generously helping each other and others to do agile right.

Finally, we must thank every member of the Berez, Elk, and Rigby families for their patience and support in this process. As we cloistered ourselves to focus on researching and writing late at night and over weekends (sometimes even during holidays), our families never wavered in their encouragement or love for us. No teams matter more than our family teams.

About the Authors

DARRELL RIGBY is a Boston-based partner and head of Bain & Company's Global Innovation and Agile practices. He is also the former head of Bain's Global Retail practice. Over forty-two years of consulting, Mr. Rigby has led assignments in a wide variety of industries, including innovative growth strategies for more than one hundred of the world's leading companies.

SARAH ELK is head of Bain & Company's Global Operating Model practice. She has driven transformational change with many iconic companies over twenty years of consulting. She believes in possibility and is passionate about unleashing human potential as companies transform. She resides in the Chicago area with her husband and four children.

STEVE BEREZ first joined Bain & Company in 1980 and has been with the firm for a total of twenty-eight years. He is a founder of Bain's Enterprise Technology practice and was until recently its Americas head. Over the past decade, Mr. Berez has helped dozens of firms around the world improve the speed, agility, and effectiveness of their technology-based innovation. He lives in Boston and is inspired by his wife and their two children.